STUDY GUIDE

for

The Enjoyment of Music

Seventh Edition

STUDY GUIDE
for

The Enjoyment of Music

Seventh Edition

KRISTINE FORNEY
California State University, Long Beach

W. W. NORTON & COMPANY
New York • London

Printed in the United States of America.
Seventh Edition

ISBN: 0-393-96684-4

W. W. Norton & Company, Inc., 500 Fifth Avenue, New York, N.Y. 10110
W. W. Norton & Company Ltd., 10 Coptic Street, London WC1A 1PU

5 6 7 8 9 0

Contents

Preface

This Study Guide, which accompanies *The Enjoyment of Music*, Seventh Edition, is designed to help you get the most out of your music studies by reinforcing the materials in the text and by guiding you in the exploration of new musical styles. This workbook is organized to coincide with the Chronological and Shorter versions of the text; however, it is equally usable with the Standard version. Exercises throughout the guide are keyed to chapters, Listening Guides (LG), and Cultural Perspectives (CP) in all versions of the text. In this Guide you will find the following:

a. Thirty-nine exercises entitled "Reviewing," based on the most important terms, concepts, and historical information in the text. These exercises test your knowledge and understanding through objective questions (multiple choice, true or false, matching, and short answer). For some, you are asked to consider an idea and give your opinion. The questions are designed to help you prepare for exams and quizzes. Your instructor may assign review exercises to be completed and turned in (you will notice that the pages are perforated for easy removal) or may suggest that you do them on your own to reinforce your studying.

b. Thirty-seven exercises entitled "Listening" that help guide your study of the musical selections outlined in the text (in Listening Guides) and included on the recording set. Note that questions about works that are included **only** on the larger 8-CD or 8-cassette set of *The Norton Recordings* (which accompanies the Chronological and Standard versions) have an asterisk (*) next to them; if you are using the Shorter text and 3-CD or 3-cassette set of recordings, you should skip these. The questions ask for you to describe certain musical elements you hear, and also review the history and form of each work. Before completing these listening exercises, you should read about the work and listen to it while following the Listening Guide in the text.

c. Twenty-seven studies entitled "Exploring" that review your understanding of the information presented in the Cultural Perspectives throughout the text. These guides are designed to broaden your knowledge of traditional, popular, and certain non-Western musics by opening windows to these cultures and helping you learn how they have influenced or been influenced by Western art music. For each of these exercises, there is a suggested outside assignment (generally listening) that allows you some freedom to explore another style of music and write about it. The exercises can be assigned by the instructor as either required or extra-credit work, or you can decide which you are most interested in doing outside of class.

d. Twelve Music Activities that allow you more direct and sometimes "hands-on" experience with music. These can be assigned to you to do alone or in small groups (study groups or discussion sections). The introduction to this section on page 207 provides more information about these guides.

e. Five Concert Report Outlines, which can be completed during or after a concert. Since most music appreciation classes require concert attendance and written reports, these outlines may be completed and turned in or may serve as an outline for a prose report, depending on course requirements. The introduction to this section on page 233 lists the five different outlines and tells you what types of music each should be used for. This is followed by a sample completed outline based on a hypothetical concert, and a sample prose report as well.

This Study Guide also includes two surveys: one to complete at the beginning of the course and one to fill out at its close. Instructors may wish to collect these surveys to familiarize themselves with the musical tastes and experiences of their students, or you may use them to gauge how your own tastes and experiences have changed as a result of taking the class, reading *The Enjoyment of Music* text, and using the accompanying materials.

I am indebted to Michael Ochs and Claire Brook of W. W. Norton for their careful reading and critique of this guide, and to Susan Gaustad for her expert copyediting. I also wish to express my sincere appreciation to the many faculty who have offered helpful suggestions for this edition of the guide, to my colleagues at California State University, Long Beach, for their contributions and unflagging loyalty, and to the many students on whom I have tried out these exercises. Through the use of these materials, they arrived, as I hope you will, at a new enjoyment of music.

Kristine Forney

Note on Abbreviations

Throughout this Study Guide, the following abbreviations are used:

C   = Chronological version of *The Enjoyment of Music,* 7th ed.
Sh = Shorter version of the text
S   = Standard version of the text
LG = Listening Guide
CP = Cultural Perspective
*   = For use with C, S, 8-CD, or 8-cassette versions only

References to the three different versions of the book are given by chapter number; use the Table of Contents to locate the correct pages in the text. References to Listening Guides are given by LG numbers and to Cultural Perspectives by CP numbers. For quick access to these pages in the text, consult the Tables of Cultural Perspectives and Listening Guides in the front of your book. A Table of Listening Guides and Recordings is printed inside the cover of your text to help you locate the musical selections on whichever recording package you are using.

NAME _____ DATE _____ CLASS _____

Pre-Course Survey

Level: ___ Freshman ___ Sophomore ___ Junior ___ Senior ___ Grad

___ High school ___ Adult education Other _____

Major (or undeclared): _____

Minor area (or undeclared): _____

Why did you take this course?

___ general education credit ___ free elective ___ enjoy music

___ required for major ___ convenient time ___ instructor

How did you hear about this course?

___ recommended by adviser ___ recommended by student(s)

___ found on my own ___ other _____

MUSICAL TASTES:

Do you listen to music: ___ frequently? ___ sometimes?

___ only a little? ___ never?

What music listening equipment do you have available?

___ radio ___ cassette ___ CD player ___ CD-ROM drive

___ laser disc ___ car stereo other _____

What styles of music do you prefer to listen to?

_____

_____

Name three favorite compositions of any type.

Title   Composer (or performer)

_____

_____

_____

List three favorite performers or performing groups.

_____

_____

_____

Do you attend live concerts? ___ yes ___ no

If yes, name one you particularly enjoyed.

_____

MUSICAL BACKGROUND: Check the musical experiences that apply.

___ Played an instrument   Which instrument? _____

___ Took music lessons   How many years? _____

___ Played or sang in a group

   ___ band   ___ orchestra   ___ chorus   ___ rock band

   ___ musical theater   ___ jazz ensemble   ___ church choir

   other _____

___ Studied music theory

___ Studied music appreciation/history

Which of the following concerts have you attended? Name the group or a work performed, if you remember.

___ orchestra _____

___ opera _____

___ musical _____

___ ballet _____

___ concert band _____

___ jazz band _____

___ rock band _____

___ choir/chorus _____

___ chamber group _____

___ solo recital _____

___ world music _____

___ other _____

What do you hope to learn in this course? _____

_____

_____

_____

Other comments: _____

_____

STUDY GUIDE

for

The Enjoyment of Music

Seventh Edition

1. *Reviewing* Elements of Music: Melody and Rhythm
(Chap. 1–2 C/Sh/S)

Terms to Remember

melody	structure of melody	beat	compound meter
pitch	phrase	unaccented	sextuple
interval	cadence	accented	additive meter
range	countermelody	simple meter	upbeat
shape	rhythm	duple	syncopation
type of movement	meter	triple	polyrhythm
conjunct	measure	quadruple	nonmetric
disjunct			

Complete the following questions.

1. The distance between two different pitches is a(n) _____.

2. A _____ is a sequence of notes that is perceived as a unity.

3. A melody that moves stepwise in a connected style is called _____, while one that features many leaps is called _____.

4. The characteristic of melody that describes its direction or movement up and down is referred to as its _____ while the distance between its highest and lowest notes is called its _____.

5. A resting point in a melody is known as a(n)_____.

6. The melody of *Amazing Grace* (on p. 10 of the text) is organized into four equal parts known as _____.

7. The regular pulse and basic unit of length heard in most Western music is called the _____.

8. Those pulses that are stronger than others are known as _____, while weaker pulses are called _____.

9. The organizing factor in music that sets fixed time patterns is called

_____.

10. Meters that subdivide beats into groups of twos are called_____.

11. Meters that subdivide beats into threes are called _____.

12. The meter of the patriotic song *America the Beautiful* is best described as _____. Rather than beginning on the downbeat or first beat of the meter, it begins with a(n) _____.

13. What would be the most likely meter for a march? _____ Why?

_____

14. The rhythmic procedure that is used to temporarily upset or throw off the meter is called _____.

15. The simultaneous use of two or more rhythmic patterns is called _____. Where is this style commonly heard? _____

16. Groupings of irregular numbers of beats that add up to an overall larger pattern produces a(n) _____ meter.

17. Music with a weak or veiled beat may be considered _____.

Sing through the entire melody of the children's song *Twinkle, Twinkle, Little Star* before answering the questions below.

Twin-kle, twin-kle lit - tle star, How I won-der what you are. Up a - bove the world so high,

Like a diamond in the sky! Twin-kle, twin-kle lit - tle star, How I won-der what you are.

Check the correct answer for each.

18. Is this melody principally: ___ conjunct (connected, smooth) or ___ disjunct (disjointed, with leaps)?

19. Is the range of this melody: ___ narrow (spanning few notes) or ___ wide (spanning many notes)?

20. Is the shape of the melody: ___ wavelike or ___ a straight line?

Consider the rhythm and meter of the well-known song *Happy Birthday* and answer the following questions. Add bar lines to mark off the meter.

Text:	Hap-py	birth-	day	to	you,	
Meter:	3	1	2	3	1	2

Text:	Hap-py	birth-	day	to	you,	
Meter:	3	1	2	3	1	2

21. What meter is indicated in the example? ___ duple ___ triple ___ quadruple ___ sextuple

22. The song begins on: ___ an accented beat ___ an unaccented beat.

23. This is an example of: ___ simple meter ___ compound meter.

2

---

2. *Reviewing* Elements of Music: Harmony and Texture
(Chap. 3–4 C/Sh/S)

Terms to Remember

harmony	drone	texture	canon, round
chord	scale	monophony	inversion
scale	major	heterophony	retrograde
octave	minor	polyphony	retrograde
triad	diatonic	homophony	inversion
tonic, tonality	chromatic	counterpoint	diminution
syllables		imitation	augmentation
dissonance, consonance			

Complete the following questions.

1. The element of music that pertains to the movement and relationship of intervals and chords is _____. Is it central to Western music? _____ to all musics of the world? _____

2. What are the syllables used to identify the tones of the scale?

   <u>do</u> _____ _____ _____ _____ _____ _____ _____

3. The interval between the first and the last syllable of the scale above is called a(n) _____.

4. The interval of a fifth in syllables is do to _____.

5. Three or more tones sounded together are called a(n) _____.

6. A triad is a three-note chord built from alternate scale tones, such as

   <u>do</u> ____ ____. In numbers, it would be scale tones 1 ___ ___.

7. In the organizing system known as tonality, the first scale tone, or keynote, is known as the _____.

8. The two scales types that are commonly found in Western music from around 1650 to 1900 are _____ and _____.

9. Music built from the tones of one of the scale types above is referred to as _____, while music built from the full range of notes in the octave is referred to as _____.

10. What kind of scale would a lament probably be built on? _____

11. Unstable musical sounds in need of resolution are called

    _____. How might they sound?_____

12. Musical sounds that seem stable, not needing to resolve, are called
_____. How might they sound?_____

13. Some musics of the world make use of a supporting sustained tone
called a(n) _____, over which melodies unfold.

14. The element of music that refers to its fabric, or the interplay of its
parts, is known as _____.

15. Music with a single melodic line and no accompaniment is called
_____ texture, whereas a musical texture with a single
melody and a chordal accompaniment is called _____.

16. A musical texture that combines two or more melodic voices is known
as _____.

17. A melody combined with an ornamented version of itself produces a
texture known as _____. In what styles of music does
this frequently occur? _____

18. The art of combining two or more voices into a single texture is known
as _____. Its name means "note against note."

19. Overlapping statements of the same melody in several parts is known as
_____, producing a _____ texture.

20. A strictly ordered composition based on one voice imitating another is
called _____. A more popular form of this compositional
type is known as a(n) _____.

21. When a melody is heard backward, it is in _____.

22. When a melody is turned upside down, so that its intervals occur in the
opposite direction, the technique is called _____.

23. _____ means a melody is heard slower (twice as slow).

24. The opposite technique, in which a melody is presented faster than its
original form, is called _____.

25. Describe a hypothetical musical situation for each of the following textures:
monophonic texture (e.g.) *Happy Birthday* sung without accompaniment
homophonic texture _____

_____

polyphonic texture _____

_____

3. *Reviewing* Elements of Music: Form
(Chap. 5 C/Sh/S)

Terms to Remember

repetition	binary form	thematic development
contrast	ternary form	call and response
variation	theme, motive	ostinato
improvisation	sequence	movement

Complete the following questions.

1. The element of music representing clarity and order is _____ .

2. The two basic principles of musical structures are _____ and _____ . A third principle of form is _____ .

3. Binary form can best be outlined as _____ . Which principle of form (from question 2) is central to this scheme? _____

4. Ternary form can best be outlined as _____ . Which principles of form does this structure illustrate? _____

5. Pieces created by performers during the performance (as opposed to being precomposed) are based on _____ . In which styles of music is this common? _____

6. A melody used as a building block is called a(n) _____ . This melody can be broken up into _____ , and it can be treated in _____ , where the idea is repeated at another pitch level.

7. Expansion of a theme is called _____ .

8. The repetitive singing style in which a leader is imitated by a group of followers is called _____ .

9. The structural procedure whereby a short melodic, rhythmic, or harmonic pattern is repeated is called _____ .

10. The self-contained sections of a large-scale work are called _____ .

11. Review the illustration on page 28 of the text that shows binary and ternary form in architecture. Describe other instances in which both forms are found in our lives, either natural or man-made. Remember that ternary is not just a three-part form, but a symmetrical one,

reflecting a departure or contrasting middle section followed by a
return to the opening.

_____

_____

_____

_____

_____

Consider the melody of the traditional song *On Top of Old Smoky,* and answer
the questions below.

On top of old Smo - ky,_____ All cov-ered with snow,_____ I

lost my true lov - er,_____ By court - in' too slow._____

12. How many musical phrases are shown in this melody?

____ 1 ____ 2 ____ 3 ____ 4

13. Are they symmetrical (the same length)?_____

14. Does the phrase beginning in measure 4 (on the last beat) provide

____ repetition or

____ contrast?

15. Does the second half of the melody

_____ repeat the first half exactly or

_____ present a variation of the first half?

16. Compare the pitches in measures 5 and 13 of this melody.
    What relationship do they have to each other?

____ retrograde   ____ inversion

____ retrograde inversion   ____ augmentation

4. *Reviewing* Elements of Music: Tempo and Dynamics
(Chap. 6 C/Sh/S)

Terms to Remember

tempo

  accelerando   meno

  adagio   moderato

  allegro   molto

  andante   non troppo

  a tempo   poco

  grave   presto

  largo   ritardando

            vivace

dynamics

  crescendo

  decrescendo

  diminuendo

  forte

  fortissimo

  mezzo piano

  mezzo forte

  piano

  pianissimo

  sforzando

Complete the following questions.

1. The standard Italian term for a fast, cheerful tempo is _____.

2. The Italian modifier meaning "not too much" is _____.

3. What tempo is even faster than that of question 1? _____

4. A slow tempo at pace of walking is _____

5. The indication to become gradually slower is _____,

  to become gradually faster is _____.

6. A return to the original tempo would be indicated _____.

7. A tempo marking of *poco a poco adagio* means _____.

8. A tempo of *molto vivace* would be best translated as _____.

9. The dynamic marking for soft is _____ and for loud, _____.

10. Growing gradually louder would be indicated by _____;

  growing gradually softer is indicated by _____.

11. A sudden stress or accent might be called for by a _____.

True or False

____ 12. Dynamics in music can affect our emotional reactions.

____ 13. Nineteenth-century musical scores generally lack indications for dynamics or tempo.

____ 14. A change in volume from **mp** to *f* would be indicated by a *diminuendo*.

_____ 15. The softest dynamic marking ever used is **_pp_**.

_____ 16. Tempo and dynamics contribute to the overall musical expression of a piece.

Consider the musical score below from Clara Schumann's Scherzo, Op. 10, a solo piano work we will study later, and answer the following questions about the tempo and dynamic markings on the music.

17. The tempo marking of *Presto* indicates _____.

18. The dynamic level at the opening (**_p_**) means _____.

19. In measure 5, the marking **_mf_** indicates _____.

20. The sign in the next measure (>) indicates a(n) _____,

    meaning to _____.

21. At the end of the second line, the marking **_sf_** means _____,

    indicating the pianist should _____.

---

5. *Reviewing* World Musical Instruments, Ensembles, and Their Context (Chap. 7–10 C/Sh/S)

Match the following instruments with their category of sound production (use choices on the right as many times as needed).

_____ 1. gourd rattle   a. aerophone

_____ 2. Japanese koto   b. chordophone

_____ 3. bagpipe   c. idiophone

_____ 4. Indian sitar   d. membranophone

_____ 5. Indian tabla

_____ 6. gong

Complete the following questions.

7. The instrument category that includes horns and flutes is _____.

8. The instrument category that produces sound from the substance of the instrument as it is rubbed, struck, or shaken is _____.

9. _____ describes any instrument sounded from a tightly stretched skin that is struck, rubbed, or plucked.

10. _____ describes an instrument that produces sound from a vibrating string stretched between two points. It can be sounded by two means: _____ and _____.

11. Name two modern Western instruments of Middle Eastern origin:

a. _____ b. _____

True or False

_____ 12. The gong is widely used throughout Africa.

_____ 13. Members of the xylophone family are used in Southeast Asia and Africa.

_____ 14. Trumpets and horns were used in the ancient world.

_____ 15. The tom-tom is a type of gong of African origin.

_____ 16. Chamber groups combining strings and percussion are common in India.

_____ 17. The gamelan is a type of orchestra in Indonesia.

_____ 18. Gagaku is the name of an African drum.

_____ 19. Turkish Janissary bands included wind and percussion instruments.

_____ 20. All ensembles around the world make use of a conductor.

_____ 21. In some cultures, women's voices are preferred for certain styles of music.

_____ 22. A koto is a bowed string instrument from India.

_____ 23. The sitar is used in classical music from India.

_____ 24. Music serves different functions in different societies.

_____ 25. Musical genres, or categories of music, are the same in all societies.

_____ 26. Vocal timbre, or tone quality, varies from culture to culture, based on differing preferences.

_____ 27. In modern times, all music is notated, or written down.

_____ 28. Oral transmission involves performance without notation.

_____ 29. Classical (art) music is never influenced by traditional or popular music.

_____ 30. Crossover refers to a kind of music notation.

31. Locate a recording of a Japanese koto or Indian sitar, listen to several selections, and describe the sound of the instrument below.
(Use the recording notes to help you answer the following questions.)

Recording title: _____

Instrument(s): _____

Description: _____

_____

_____

_____

Is this ___ traditional, ___ popular, or ___ classical music?

What function does this style play in its native society?

_____

_____

_____

6. *Reviewing* Western Orchestral Instruments
(Chap. 8 C/Sh/S)

Identify each of the instruments pictured below in four ways: its name, chosen from column I; its instrument family, from column II; its means of sound production, from column III; and its world instrument category, from column IV.

I. INSTRUMENT
  a. bassoon
  b. clarinet
  c. double bass
  d. flute
  e. French horn
  f. oboe
  g. saxophone
  h. timpani
  i. trombone
  j. trumpet
  k. tuba
  l. violin

II. FAMILY
  m. brass
  n. percussion
  o. strings
  p. woodwinds

IV. CATEGORY
  w. aerophones
  x. chordophones
  y. idiophones
  z. membranophones

III. SOUND PRODUCTION
  q. blown double reed
  r. blown single reed
  s. bowed string
  t. struck with mallets
  u. air column divided across hole
  v. lips buzzing into mouthpiece

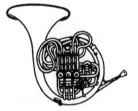

1. Instrument: _l_
   Family: _o_
   Production: _s_
   Category: _x_

2. Instrument: ___
   Family: ___
   Production: ___
   Category: ___

3. Instrument: ___
   Family: ___
   Production: ___
   Category: ___

4. Instrument: ___
   Family: ___
   Production: ___
   Category: ___

5. Instrument: ___
   Family: ___
   Production: ___
   Category: ___

6. Instrument: ___
   Family: ___
   Production: ___
   Category: ___

7. Instrument: ___
   Family: ___
   Production: ___
   Category: ___

8. Instrument: ___
   Family: ___
   Production: ___
   Category: ___

9. Instrument: ___
   Family: ___
   Production: ___
   Category: ___

10. Instrument: ___
    Family: ___
    Production: ___
    Category: ___

11. Instrument: ___
    Family: ___
    Production: ___
    Category: ___

12. Instrument: ___
    Family: ___
    Production: ___
    Category: ___

13. Which instruments do you find are difficult to tell apart?

   _____

   _____

14. Which do you find easy to distinguish?

   _____

   _____

There are several pieces of music that feature the sounds of the instruments (in addition to Britten's *Young Person's Guide to the Orchestra*, discussed in Chapter 9 and Listening Guide 1). One of these is Sergei Prokofiev's *Peter and the Wolf*.

15. Listen to this work, and describe the roles given to the instruments.

   _____

   _____

   _____

   _____

7. *Reviewing* Musical Instruments and Ensembles
(Chap. 7–9 C/Sh/S)

Terms to Remember

a cappella	embouchure	plucked
alto	jazz band	register
baritone	madrigal choir	soprano
bass	mezzo-soprano	string quartet
bowed	orchestra	tenor
chamber music	part songs	timbre
concert band	piano quartet	unpitched
conductor	pitch	volume
duration	pitched	woodwind quintet

Complete the following questions.

1. The four qualities of any musical sound are _____,

   _____, _____, and _____.

2. The distinctive sound of each instrument is its _____.

3. List the three standard voice parts for women (highest to lowest).

   _____ _____ _____

4. List the three standard voice parts for men.

   _____ _____ _____

5. The two categories of orchestral string instruments, grouped by the way

   they are played, are _____ and _____.

   Name an instrument for each: _____ and _____

6. The two categories of percussion instruments are _____ and

   _____. Examples: _____ and _____

7. The lips, lower facial muscles, and jaw are referred to as a wind player's

   _____.

8. _____ refers to music sung without accompaniment.

9. Small ensembles with one musician per part play _____.

10. The standard ensemble consisting of 2 violins, 1 viola, and 1 cello is

    known as a(n) _____.

11. A chamber ensemble that includes flute, oboe, clarinet, French horn,

    and bassoon is known as a(n) _____.

12. One chamber ensemble of piano and strings is the _____.

13. A large musical ensemble made up predominantly of winds and percussion is the _____.

14. An ensemble made up of sections of reed, brass, and rhythm instruments that plays popular music is the _____.

15. The person who beats time to help keep large ensembles together is known as a(n) _____.

Match the following string effects with their definitions on the right.

_____ 16. pizzicato   a. a rapid alternation from one tone to the one above it

_____ 17. trill   b. muffling the sound by a small attachment on the bridge

_____ 18. vibrato   c. plucking the string with the finger

_____ 19. muting   d. playing two notes at one time

_____ 20. staccato   e. a slide on the string while bowing

_____ 21. double stopping   f. a short, detached style of playing

_____ 22. glissando   g. throbbing effect produced by slightly wiggling the finger while bowing

23. Watch a conductor in action (in a live performance or on a video or TV broadcast). Describe his or her hand motions and other body language as it relates to the performance.

_____

_____

_____

_____

_____

_____

_____

_____

---
8. *Listening* **Britten's** *Young Person's Guide to the Orchestra*
(**LG** 1 C/Sh/S)

Locate a recording (or the video) of *The Young Person's Guide to the Orchestra*
(it is on the 8-CD and 8-cassette set accompanying your textbook). Some
recordings have narration, and others do not. Decide whether you need the
narration to help you identify the instruments. Follow Listening Guide 1
while listening, then answer the questions below.

THEME

1. What was Britten's source for the theme (main melody) of this work?

   _____

2. Describe the character of the theme in your own words.

   _____

3. How does the composer firmly establish this melody for the listener?

   _____

4. Can you differentiate between the sounds of each instrument family?

   _____ Describe in your own words the timbre, or distinctive

   sound, of each family below.

   Woodwinds: _____

   Brass: _____

   Strings: _____

   Percussion: _____

VARIATIONS After the statements of the theme by each instrument family,
Britten begins a series of variations on the theme.

5. How would you define a variation on a musical theme?

   _____

   _____

6. Can you recognize the theme throughout the variations? _____

7. Can you distinguish the solo instrument over those that are playing the

   accompaniment?_____

8. Which woodwind instruments do you find easy to identify?

_____

Which are difficult? _____

9. Which string instruments do you find easy to identify?

_____

Which are difficult?_____

10. Which brass instruments do you find easy to identify?

_____

Which are difficult?_____

11. Of the percussion instruments heard, which have a definite pitch?

_____

Which are unpitched? _____

FUGUE Use the last section of the work as a final review of the instruments. Here each instrument is heard-in a very quick statement of a new theme or melody.

12. Knowing the range an instrument plays in will help you distinguish it from another family member whose timbre is similar. Arrange the instruments of each family from highest to lowest, as they are heard in both the variations and the fugue. Assign number 1 to the highest family member, 2 to the next highest, and so on.

___ bassoon	___ viola	___ French horn
___ piccolo	___ cello	___ tuba
___ clarinet	___ violin	___ trumpet
___ flute	___ double bass	___ trombone

13. How does Britten use imitation in this section of the piece?

_____

14. Where is the climax of the work? _____

_____

9. *Reviewing* Hearing Musical Styles
(Trans. I C/Sh/S)

Complete the following questions.

1. What determines the style of any work of art?

   _____

   _____

2. Specifically, what determines the style of a musical work?

   _____

   _____

   _____

3. What are some factors that make certain styles of non-Western music
   sound different to us from more familiar music?

   _____

   _____

   _____

   _____

4. Style is also what makes popular and classical music sound different.
   List some types of popular music that you think represent differing styles.

   _____

   _____

   _____

   _____

5. Does the development of music in other world cultures follow the style
   periods of Western music? _____
   Explain your answer.

   _____

   _____

   _____

6. Place the following Western style periods in chronological order by numbering them from 1 (the earliest) to 6 (the latest) in the left column. Give the approximate dates of each era in the right column.

Era	Dates
____ Baroque	_____
____ Middle Ages	_____
____ Romantic	_____
____ Twentieth century	_____
____ Classical	_____
____ Renaissance	_____

7. Do the dates of musical periods coincide precisely with the dates of literary or artistic style periods? ____ yes ____ no ____ don't know

8. Why or why not?

_____

_____

_____

9. Why do scholars have difficulty agreeing about when one musical style period ends and the next one begins?

_____

_____

_____

_____

_____

10. *Reviewing* Music in the Middle Ages
(Chap. 11–13 C/Sh; 49–51 S)

Sacred Music

True or False

_____ 1. Medieval monasteries played a central role in the preservation of knowledge from earlier cultures.

_____ 2. The church was especially important in shaping secular music of early times.

_____ 3. Hildegard of Bingen was an abbess who wrote church music.

_____ 4. Much music is left to us today from Greek and Roman civilizations.

_____ 5. The early music of the Christian church was influenced by Hebrew music.

_____ 6. Early musical notation, called neumes, developed as a memory tool for singers who learned chants orally.

_____ 7. The chants of the church used only the major and minor scale patterns found in later music.

_____ 8. The Mass of the Roman Catholic Church is celebrated daily and includes a Proper, which is appropriate to the feast for that day, as well as the Ordinary, which remains the same for all feast days.

_____ 9. The Notre Dame school is renowned for early polyphonic writing called organum.

_____ 10. Léonin and Pérotin are important composers from the St. Peter's school of organum in Rome.

_____ 11. The cloistered life in the Middle Ages was open only to men.

_____ 12. People who entered religious orders had a demanding life-style.

Complete the following sentences.

13. The _____ is the most solemn service of the Roman Catholic Church.

14. The body of music for the Roman Catholic Church is called

_____.

15. The various scale patterns used in Western music in the Middle Ages are known as _____.

16. Music performed with exchanges between a soloist and chorus is said to be _____.

Secular Music

Match the following types of musician with descriptions on the right.

_____ 17. trouvère   a. female poet-musician from France

_____ 18. troubadour   b. poet-musician of northern France

_____ 19. jongleur   c. German singer of courtly love

_____ 20. trobairitz   d. poet-musician of southern France

_____ 21. Minnesinger   e. wandering actor-singer

Multiple Choice

_____ 22. The art of the troubadours and trouvères included:
- a. laments and love songs.
- b. political and war songs.
- c. dance songs.
- d. all of the above.

_____ 23. Which was <u>not</u> an activity associated with secular music in Medieval society?
- a. dancing and dinner entertainment
- b. devotional services
- c. jousts and tournaments
- d. military and civic events

_____ 24. Which factor did <u>not</u> contribute significantly to the rise in the status of women in the Middle Ages?
- a. the cults of Marian worship
- b. the age of chivalry
- c. the love songs of court minstrels
- d. the attitudes of feudal society

25. What were the principal values during the age of chivalry? Which of these are valid today?

_____

_____

_____

26. Cite a popular song of today that echoes the sentiments of unrequited love heard in Medieval songs.

_____

| 11. *Exploring* **The Changing Face of Patronage**
(**CP** 1 C/Sh; 9 S) |

Complete the following questions.

1. What is a patron? _____

_____

2. In the Middle Ages, which two institutions were the most supportive

 patrons of music?

 a. _____ b. _____

3. Name three employment possibilities for musicians in the Middle Ages:

 a. _____ b. _____ c. _____

4. What functions did music serve at courts in early times?

_____

_____

5. Name a noblewoman who was a noted patron of music.

_____

6. What role did the middle class play in the sixteenth century in the

 support of music? _____

_____

7. Which eighteenth-century composer lived comfortably under the

 patronage system? _____ Which composer

 was ill-suited to the system? _____

8. Name three means of employment for musicians today.

 a. _____ b. _____ c. _____

9. What types of patrons exist today for music and the arts?

_____

_____

10. Name a government agency that sponsors music and the arts.

_____

Essay: What role does the private individual (like you) play as a supporter of the arts? In what ways can individuals function as patrons?

_____

_____

_____

_____

_____

_____

_____

_____

_____

_____

_____

_____

_____

_____

_____

_____

_____

_____

_____

_____

_____

_____

_____

_____

_____

_____

_____

_____

_____

13. *Exploring* Influence on the Early Christian Church
(CP 2 C/Sh; 10 S)

1. List three Judaic traditions or beliefs that were retained by the early Christian church.

    a. _____

    b. _____

    c. _____

2. Which large section of the Bible serves both Judaism and Christianity today? _____

3. Which specific book of the Bible is important to both religions?

    _____

    Describe this book. _____

    _____

    _____

4. What is a cantor? _____

5. What is a synagogue?_____

6. Describe responsorial singing. _____

    _____

    _____

7. In which church(es) is responsorial singing used?

    _____

8. Which famous European Roman Catholic church shows Byzantine architectural features? _____

9. Why did the early Christian church avoid using instruments in its services? _____

    _____

    _____

10. If a text is in the vernacular, in which language is it?

    _____

Music listening assignment: Find a recording of Jewish cantorial music in your library (or ask your instructor for one from the Music Example Bank). Listen and compare its singing style and melodic characteristics with Gregorian chant (for example, *Haec dies,* on your recordings).

---

14. *Listening* Medieval Secular Music
   Machaut: *Hareu! hareu! le feu/Helas!/Obediens* (**LG** 5 C; 3 Sh; 33 S)
   * Moniot d'Arras: *Ce fut en mai* (**LG** 4 C; 32 S)
   * Anonymous: Saltarello (**LG** 6 C; 34 S)

Listen to the Machaut motet while following the Listening Guide, and answer the questions below.

1. This motet represents: ___ secular music or ___ sacred music.

2. The era it represents is: ___ Ars Antiqua or ___ Ars Nova.

3. The motet is based on: ___ a plainsong ostinato or ___ a secular song.

4. The motet's structure is: ___ isorhythmic or ___ freely composed.

5. The motet is: ___ based on a single Latin text or

   ___ based on polytextual love songs.

6. The top voice is called: ___ the triplum or ___ the Tenor.

7. The middle voice is called: ___ the duplum or ___ the Tenor.

8. The slowest moving voice is: ___ the triplum or ___ the Tenor.

9. The motet uses the technique of: ___ retrograde or ___ diminution.

10. The composer was: ___ a troubadour or ___ a courtier and cleric.

11. The Tenor is played on: ___ a lute or ___ a sackbut.

12. What accounts for the complexity you hear in this work?

   _____

   _____

13. What holds the work together structurally?_____

   _____

*Comparing Two Medieval Secular Works

   a. Moniot d'Arras: *Ce fut en mai*
   b. Anonymous: Saltarello

Listen to the two works above, following the Listening Guides. In the next seven questions, write the letter of the work (a or b) next to each characteristic that applies; more than one answer may be appropriate.

____ 14. The form of the piece is a strophic chanson of five verses, each with an elaborate rhyme scheme.

____ 15. Instrumental improvisation is central to the performance of this work.

_____ 16. The piece portrays the character of a lively, leaping dance.

_____ 17. The work is a monophonic song that is often performed with improvised instrumental accompaniment.

_____ 18. The work can appropriately be performed with instruments of the loud, or outdoor, category.

_____ 19. The work is written by one of the last of the trouvères.

_____ 20. The work has a monophonic texture.

Early Instruments

_____ *21. The melody instrument heard in the Saltarello is a:
   a. sackbut.
   b. shawm.
   c. lute.

_____ 22. The tabor is a:
   a. brass instrument.
   b. percussion instrument.
   c. woodwind instrument.

_____ 23. _____ instruments were used for outdoor events.
   a. Bas (soft)
   b. Haut (loud)
   c. Grand (large)

_____ 24. Which is not a type of early organ?
   a. portative
   b. positive
   c. virginal

_____ *25. The instruments heard in *Ce fut en mai* are:
   a. woodwinds.
   b. strings.
   c. brass.

26. Which early instruments have modern counterparts? Which do not?

_____

_____

_____

_____

---

15. *Exploring* Opening Doors to the East
(**CP** 3 C/Sh; 11 S)

Complete the following questions.

1. What was the purpose of the Crusades? _____

   _____

   In which centuries did they take place? _____

2. What modern geographical locale was the goal of the crusaders?

   _____

3. What military skills did Europeans learn from their enemies?

   _____

   _____

4. What types of knowledge were acquired from the Arab world?

   _____

   _____

5. Name three ways in which music was influenced by the

   Eastern world:

   a. _____

   b. _____

   c. _____

6. What Chinese ruler welcomed Marco Polo into his empire?

   _____

   In which century?_____

7. What technical skills did Marco Polo and his explorers bring to western

   Europe from China? _____

   _____

8. What can we deduce from Polo's writings about the Tartars' use of

   music? _____

   _____

9. What religion was established in China during this era?

   _____

Essay: Discuss ways in which early historical encounters between Eastern and Western peoples contributed to the global awareness of today's society.

_____

_____

_____

_____

_____

_____

_____

_____

_____

_____

_____

_____

Music listening assignment: Listen to the Medieval Saltarello discussed in your book (or another Medieval instrumental dance), and comment on how it might have been influenced by early cultural interactions. (Note: The Saltarello may be found on the 8-cassette or 8-CD recording set.)

_____

_____

_____

_____

_____

_____

_____

_____

_____

_____

_____

_____

16. *Reviewing* The Renaissance Spirit
(Chap. 14 C/Sh; 52 S)

1. The Renaissance represents: (check one)
   ___ a. a sudden rebirth in learning and the arts or
   ___ b. an increased awareness of the cultures of learned civilizations.

2. The new era was characterized by:
   ___ a. an increased secular orientation or
   ___ b. a complete religious orientation.

3. It was an age of:
   ___ a. scientific and intellectual inquiry or
   ___ b. acceptance of faith and authority.

4. Check all those historical events that took place during the Renaissance:
   ___ a. the discovery of the New World
   ___ b. the invention of printing
   ___ c. the writing of the Magna Carta
   ___ d. the fall of the Roman Empire
   ___ e. the Protestant Reformation
   ___ f. the writing of the U.S. Constitution

5. Match the following well-known Renaissance personalities with their description on the right:

   ____ Michelangelo   a. Italian scientist and astronomer

   ____ Erasmus   b. German religious reformer

   ____ Machiavelli   c. Italian statesman

   ____ Galileo   d. Italian painter and sculptor

   ____ Martin Luther   e. Italian patroness of the arts

   ____ Isabella d'Este   f. Dutch humanist writer

6. Name two great works of art created during the Renaissance (check text illustrations for examples).

   Artist   Work of art

   _____

   _____

7. What were some of the philosophical developments of the Renaissance that moved society forward toward today's culture?

   _____

   _____

The Musician in Society

8. The ways in which musicians made their living in the Renaissance are similar to today's. For each of the following supporting institutions, list one specific use of music in the Renaissance and a parallel activity today.

	Renaissance	Modern day
Church:		
Civic:		
Amateur music making:		
Aristocratic courts:		
Entertainment events:		

9. What effect did the rise of a new middle class of merchants have on the commerce of music?

_____

_____

10. What roles did women play in music during the Renaissance era?

_____

_____

Renaissance Musical Style

True or False

_____ 11. The Renaissance saw the rise of solo instrumental music alongside the great vocal forms.

_____ 12. An a cappella performance of a vocal work might feature improvised instrumental accompaniment.

_____ 13. The predominant texture of Renaissance vocal music was imitative polyphony.

_____ 14. Expressive musical devices were frequently linked to the text in Renaissance music.

_____ 15. The use of a cantus firmus, or fixed melody, was abandoned in the Renaissance in favor of freer forms.

_____ 16. Renaissance music reflects a new taste for duple meter.

17. *Exploring* When the Old World Meets the New World
(**CP** 4 C/Sh; 12 S)

Complete the following questions.

1. During which historical era did Columbus explore the New World?

   _____

2. What musical characteristics did early explorers note about the singing
   of Native Americans? _____

   _____

3. What types of instruments did Europeans note were in use by Native
   Americans? _____

4. Describe how one of these was made. _____

   _____

   _____

5. Name three functions that music played in Native American society.

   a. _____

   b. _____

   c. _____

6. Describe call-and-response singing. _____

   _____

   _____

7. What is a vocable?_____

8. Explain how music is preserved by oral tradition.

   _____

   _____

   _____

9. What music is preserved today through oral tradition?

   _____

   _____

Music listening assignment: Find an example of Native American ceremonial music (preferably an "authentic" or field recording) in your college library (or ask your instructor for one from the Music Example Bank). Listen to it, and describe the musical style in your own words. Consider vocal timbre, singing styles, melodic and rhythmic characteristics (range, shape, how it moves), and instruments used.

_____

_____

_____

_____

_____

_____

_____

_____

_____

_____

_____

_____

_____

_____

_____

_____

_____

_____

_____

What was your reaction to the musical example?

_____

_____

_____

---

18. *Reviewing* **Music in the Renaissance Era**
(Chap. 15–16 C/Sh; 53–54 S)

Sacred Music

Multiple Choice

_____ 1. Which of the following was *not* sung in the Roman Catholic
Church?
   a. chansons
   b. motets
   c. masses

_____ 2. Which of the following makes up the Ordinary of the Mass?
   a. Introit, Gradual, Communion, Ite missa est
   b. Kyrie, Gloria, Credo, Sanctus, Agnus Dei
   c. Kyrie, Gloria, Collect, Epistle, Gradual

_____ 3. Which of the following movements of the mass have three-part
text and musical structures?
   a. Kyrie and Gloria
   b. Sanctus and Agnus Dei
   c. Kyrie and Agnus Dei

_____ 4. Which of the following is <u>not</u> typical of the Renaissance motet?
   a. multivoiced, sometimes based on a chant
   b. Latin texts, often in praise of the Virgin Mary
   c. monophonic, and sung in the vernacular

_____ 5. Which of the following was <u>not</u> recommended by the Council of
Trent?
   a. Remove secularisms from Church music
   b. Use more instruments in Church music
   c. Make the words more understandable

_____ 6. The Catholic Church's reform movement toward piety was:
   a. the Reformation.
   b. the Counter-Reformation.
   c. the Ordinary.

Composers of Sacred Music

True or False

_____ 7. Guillaume Dufay made use of cantus firmus technique in his masses.

_____ 8. Josquin spent his entire productive career in northern Europe.

_____ 9. Palestrina's patrons included several popes.

_____ 10. Palestrina was a Burgundian composer.

_____ 11. Josquin's music was influenced by humanism.

35

Secular Music

True or False

_____ 12. The principal forms of Renaissance secular music were the chanson and the anthem.

_____ 13. Women were barred from secular music-making activities in the Renaissance.

_____ 14. The madrigal flourished principally in France.

_____ 15. The Burgundian chanson was highly structured, based on fixed text forms.

_____ 16. The texts of the chanson and the madrigal dealt largely with love, both courtly and profane.

_____ 17. Instrumental music making was a feature of home entertainment.

_____ 18. Instruments were used exclusively for the dance and never with voices in the Renaissance.

_____ 19. Specific instruments were rarely called for in Renaissance music.

_____ 20. Instruments were divided into loud and soft categories, their use based on the occasion.

_____ 21. Renaissance composers normally wrote the texts they set to music.

Match the dance types below with the correct description on the right.

_____ 22. pavane   a. an Italian jumping dance

_____ 23. gagliard   b. a German dance in moderate duple meter

_____ 24. allemande   c. a slow, stately processional dance

_____ 25. saltarello   d. a quick French dance

26. What was the *Concerto delle donne*?

_____

27. What was new and remarkable about their singing style?

_____

_____

> **19. *Listening* Burgundian Music** (Dufay and Ockeghem)*
> * Dufay: *L'homme armé* Mass, Kyrie (**LG** 7 C; 35 S)
> * Ockeghem: *L'autre d'antan* (**LG** 10 C; 38 S)

*Listen to the early Renaissance mass movement by Dufay, and answer the following questions.

1. For how many voice parts is this mass set? _____

2. The Kyrie is the first musical movement of the _____ of the Mass.

3. What is the cantus firmus (fixed song) on which this mass is set?

_____

Can you hear the cantus firmus in the work? _____

4. What is the overall form of the movement? _____

5. How does the text contribute to shaping the form? _____

_____

6. What is the predominant texture of the movement? _____

_____

7. In which meter is this movement set? _____

8. Does the harmony sound hollow or full? _____

Explain your answer. _____

_____

9. How does the composer create variety in his setting of the work?

_____

_____

10. Why did the Catholic Church object to masses such as this one later in the sixteenth century?

_____

_____

*Listen to the Burgundian chanson by Ockeghem while following the Listening Guide, then answer the following questions.

11. In which century was this work written?_____

12. In which of the French fixed forms does this work fall?_____

13. How many times do you hear the refrain text in the work?

_____

14. For how many voices is this work set? _____

15. Are they all sung in your recording?_____

16. How would you characterize the texture of the chanson?

_____

17. How does its musical form rely on repetition and contrast?

_____

_____

18. Does the music sound archaic or modern to you? _____

    Explain. _____

19. How would you describe the tone or language of the love poem?

_____

_____

20. Compare the text with a popular love song of today. How is it similar or
    different?

_____

_____

_____

_____

20. *Listening* Sacred Music of Josquin and Palestrina
Josquin: *Ave Maria . . . virgo serena* (**LG** 8 C; 4 Sh; 36 S)
Palestrina: *Pope Marcellus* Mass, Gloria (**LG** 9 C; 5 Sh; 37 S)

Listen to the Josquin motet while following the Listening Guide, and answer the questions below.

1. For how many voice parts is this work set? _____

2. Whose virtues are praised in its text? _____

3. Describe the structure of the text. _____

_____

4. In which language is the text written? _____

5. What textures does Josquin employ to set off the different sections of

   the text? _____

_____

6. Is this work ____ based on a chant or ____ freely composed?

   Explain. _____

_____

7. Does this recording use ____ male voices only or ____ mixed voices?

   What voices would have been used in the Renaissance? _____

_____

8. Is this work performed ____ a cappella or ____ with accompaniment?

9. Would you say that Josquin's first priority was the music or text in this

   work? _____ Explain your answer. _____

_____

_____

10. Why is Josquin considered to be a great composer? _____

_____

Listen to the Palestrina mass movement while following the Listening Guide, and answer the questions below.

11. Is this movement part of the ____ Ordinary or ____ Proper of the Mass?

12. For how many voice parts is the mass written? _____

13. How does Palestrina create contrast in the voices and ranges heard?

_____

_____

14. Was this mass originally sung by ____ male voices or ____ mixed voices?
    Explain. _____

_____

15. Is this work performed ____ a cappella or ____ with instruments?

16. Is its harmony best described as ____ consonant or ____ dissonant?

17. Is its texture more ____ homophonic or ____ polyphonic?

18. Is its meter ____ duple or ____ triple?

19. How does he make the text clear and audible?

_____

_____

20. What musical concerns of the Council of Trent did Palestrina try to
    meet in this work? _____

_____

_____

21. Compare this work with the Josquin motet *Ave Maria . . . virgo serena.*
    Which sounds more modern to you?_____
    Explain your answer. _____

_____

_____

> **21.** *Listening* **Sixteenth-Century Secular Music**
> Marenzio: *Cantate Ninfe* (**LG** 12 C; 6 Sh; 40 S)
> Farmer: *Fair Phyllis* (**LG** 13 C; 7 Sh; 41 S)
> * Susato: Two Dances (**LG** 11 C; 39 S)

Listen to the two madrigals listed above while following the Listening Guides in the text. Answer the questions below.

1. In which country was the madrigal first developed? _____

2. How did the English madrigal differ from the Italian version?

_____

_____

_____

3. Which examples of word painting are expecially clear in the Marenzio madrigal? _____

_____

_____

4. Where is word painting clearly heard in *Fair Phyllis?*

_____

_____

5. What is rustic or pastoral about each of these madrigals?

_____

_____

6. Can you hear the shift to triple meter in *Cantate Ninfe?* _____
   What musical effect does it have? _____
   Can you hear the brief change to triple meter in *Fair Phyllis?* _____
   What is its musical effect? _____

7. Which of these madrigals is more dissonant? _____
   Where do dissonances occur? _____

8. Describe an example of word painting in a contemporary or popular musical composition.

_____

_____

_____

*Listen to the dances listed above published by Tielman Susato and answer the following questions about them.

9. When and where was Susato's famous dance collection published?

_____

10. What is the character of a ronde? _____

_____

11. What is the meter of the first dance? _____

What is its form? _____

What instruments are heard playing? _____

12. What is the meter of the second dance? _____

What is its form? _____

What instruments are heard playing? _____

13. How would you describe the timbre (color) of the regal (reed organ) heard in Ronde I? _____

14. How would you describe the timbre of the strings that play Ronde II?

_____

15. Of the instruments heard, which are still played today?

_____

22. *Reviewing* Transition to the Baroque
(Trans. II C/Sh; Trans. III S)

Fill in the answers below.

1. Giovanni Gabrieli was active as a composer at St. Mark's in

   _____.

2. One important characteristic of music at St. Mark's was the use of two

   or three choirs, called _____ singing.

3. The use of these choirs in alternation and then together is a singing

   style known as _____.

4. This style marked a change from the predominantly polyphonic texture

   of the Renaissance to a more _____ texture, in which

   the words could better be understood.

For each of the traits listed below, indicate with the appropriate letter (a or b)
the style to which it relates.

   a. Renaissance style
   b. Baroque style

____ 5. precise instruments specified

____ 6. modal harmony predominant

____ 7. a cappella vocal performance

____ 8. solo singing (monody) prevalent

____ 9. use of cantus firmus structures

____ 10. rise of opera and cantata

____ 11. chanson and madrigal as major secular forms

____ 12. establishment of major/minor tonality

____ 13. rise of public theaters

____ 14. sonata and concerto as important instrumental forms

____ 15. dance music derived from vocal works

Giovanni Gabrieli and the Motet*

*Listen to Gabrieli's motet *Plaudite, psallite* while following the Listening Guide, and answer the questions below.

16. What innovations in instrumental music are credited to Giovanni Gabrieli?

_____

_____

_____

17. What are terraced dynamics, and how are they used in the motet
    Plaudite, psallite?

_____

_____

_____

18. What musical forces (voices and instruments) were used to perform
    Plaudite, psallite?

_____

_____

19. Is the text clearly heard in this work? _____

    Explain your answer. _____

20. What musical effects do you think help to communicate the joyous
    nature of the text? _____

_____

_____

_____

23. *Reviewing* The Organization of Musical Sounds
(Chap. 17–18 C/Sh; 34–35 S)

Terms to Remember

key

scale

  chromatic

  diatonic

  major

  minor

  heptatonic

  pentatonic

  tritonic

mode

tonality

octave

half step/whole step

transposition

modulation

chords, active and rest

  triad

  tonic

  dominant

  subdominant

microtone

raga

Complete the following questions.

1. The division of the _____ is an important variable in musics around

the world. In Western music, it is divided into _____ equal half steps.

2. How many half steps make up a whole step? _____

3. The distance between C and D is a(n) _____.

4. How many half steps make up the chromatic scale? _____

5. _____ refers to the principle of organization whereby we
hear a piece of music in relation to a central tone.

6. In the chart below, mark on top the intervals (W for whole step and H for
half step) for a major scale, and on the bottom those for a minor scale.

```
        major
        scale:   W
                 / \ / \ / \ / \ / \ / \ / \
                 1   2   3   4   5   6   7   8
                 do  re  mi  fa  sol la  ti  do
        minor    \ / \ / \ / \ / \ / \ / \ /
        scale:
```

7. _____ refers to music built on the seven tones of a major or

minor scale. It is best associated with music of the _____
era.

8. _____ refers to music built on all the half steps in the octave.

It can best be associated with music of the _____ era.

9. _____ refers to a three-note scale, commonly used in certain musics of _____ (continent).

10. A five-note scale is referred to as _____ and is commonly heard in musics of _____.

11. What is a microtone? _____

_____

12. How do Western listeners generally react to microtones?

_____

13. How is a raga different from a scale? _____

_____

Where are ragas used? _____

14. A three-note chord built on alternate scale tones is called a(n)

_____. When built on the first scale tone, it is called a

_____ chord; when built on the fourth scale tone, it is called

a _____ chord; and when built on the fifth scale tone, it

is called a _____ chord.

15. The shifting of all the tones of a melody by a uniform distance is called

_____.

16. _____ refers to the passing from one key center to another within a composition.

17. Define active and rest chords, and describe how they function.

_____

_____

_____

_____

---
24. *Reviewing* **The Baroque and the Arts**
(Chap. 19–20 C/Sh; 55–56 S)

Briefly characterize each of the following in the Baroque.

  1. State of science: _____

           _____

     Name a scientist from this era. _____

  2. Focus of political power: _____

           _____

     Name a head of state from this era. _____

  3. Religious environment: _____

           _____

     What regions of Europe were Protestant? _____

           _____

  4. Style of painting: _____

           _____

     Name an artist from this era. _____

Multiple Choice

_____ 5. The origin of the term "Baroque" is probably:
       a. German, referring to something broken.
       b. Portuguese, referring to an irregularly shaped pearl.
       c. French, referring to a barge-type boat.

_____ 6. The university-based music ensemble that arose in the Baroque era is the:
       a. concert band.
       b. collegium musicum.
       c. madrigal choir.

Music in the Baroque

Complete the following questions.

  7. Opera had its origins in the experiments of a group known as the

     _____.

  8. The new style of music, or *le nuove musiche,* which features solo singing

     with instrumental accompaniment, is called _____.

9. The new accompaniment style was performed by a group of

_____ instruments whose players read from a shorthand

notation known as _____.

10. The belief that words and music were closely linked is reflected in the

_____.

11. The rise in opera was responsible for the popularity of the voice of the

_____, a male singer whose high register was preserved

through an operation at an early age.

12. The tuning system developed during the Baroque that increased the

range of harmonic possibilities was _____.

13. The shift from one volume level to another was known as

_____.

14. What was the importance of the establishment of major/minor tonality

in the Baroque? _____

_____

_____

15. What role did improvisation play in Baroque music? Who was expected

to improvise? _____

_____

_____

16. In which ways did Baroque music project a new internationalism?

_____

_____

25. *Exploring* Music and the American Religious Spirit
(**CP** 5 C/Sh; 13 S)

Complete the following questions.

1. In the seventeenth century, what religion was predominant along the

   Eastern Seaboard of the United States? _____

   in northeastern Canada? _____ in Mexico?_____

2. What was the first book printed in the American colonies?

   _____

3. Describe the singing style known as lining out: _____

   _____

   _____

4. When several embellished versions of the same melody occur

   simultaneously, we call this texture _____.

5. Name an important eighteenth-century American music teacher and

   composer: _____

6. What is a fuging tune? _____

   _____

7. What types of devotional music were sung in the nineteenth century?

   _____

   _____

   Was this music of African-Americans, whites, or both?

   _____

8. Describe gospel music. _____

   _____

   _____

9. What is contemporary Christian music? _____

   _____

   _____

Music listening assignment: Find a recording of twentieth-century devotional music (spiritual, gospel, contemporary Christian, Jewish, or comparable music) in your college library (or ask your instructor for one from the Music Example Bank). Listen to a selection, and describe its musical style (melody, rhythm, harmony, texture, form, tempo) and how it delivers a religious message.

_____

_____

_____

_____

_____

_____

_____

_____

_____

_____

_____

_____

_____

_____

_____

_____

_____

_____

_____

_____

_____

_____

_____

_____

_____

_____

_____

> ## 26. *Reviewing* Baroque Vocal Forms
> (Chap. 21–23 C/Sh; 57–59 S)

Fill in the answers below.

1. The text of an opera is called the _____ and is written by

   a(n) _____ .

2. Operas frequently open with an instrumental introduction called a(n)

   _____ .

3. Opera soloists are generally featured in two types of works: a lyrical

   song that provides the opportunity for emotional expression is called

   a(n) _____, while a more disjunct song whose rhythm is

   fitted to the inflection of the text is called a(n) _____ .

4. The term "secco" means _____, and

   the term "accompagnato" means _____. Both

   refer to types of _____ .

5. An operatic song in the form A-B-A, which allows for the soloist to

   embellish the last section, is called a(n) _____ .

6. The most important early Italian composer of operas was

   _____. His first opera was

   _____ .

7. The master of the Baroque oratorio in England was _____ .

   His most famous oratorio is _____ .

True or False

____ 8. Tragédie lyrique was a French opera style associated with Lully.

____ 9. An oratorio is a secular stage work, with sets, costumes, and
        dramatic action.

____ 10. The earliest opera plots were drawn from mythology.

____ 11. The cantata is multimovement work that features solo vocalists,
        chorus, and orchestra.

____ 12. The cantata was central to the service of the Roman Catholic
        Church.

____ 13. The masque was a forerunner of the cantata in England.

_____ 14. Many of Bach's cantatas are based on Protestant chorale or hymn tunes.

_____ 15. The oratorio features arias, recitatives, and choruses among its sections.

_____ 16. Cantatas may be based on either secular or sacred subjects.

_____ 17. Opera seria was Italian comic opera.

_____ 18. Women were not allowed to sing in opera productions.

19. What differentiates an opera from an oratorio?

_____

_____

_____

20. What differentiates a cantata from an oratorio?

_____

_____

_____

> **28.** *Listening* **Bach and the Lutheran Cantata**
> Bach: Cantata No. 80, *A Mighty Fortress Is Our God* (*Ein feste Burg ist unser Gott*),
> Nos. 1, 2, *5, 8 (**LG** 17 C; 9 Sh; 45 S)

Listen to the Bach cantata while following the Listening Guide, read about
it, and answer the following questions.

1. What is a chorale tune? _____

2. In a multivoiced setting, in which voice is the chorale tune generally

   heard? _____

3. Who wrote the chorale text *Ein feste Burg ist unser Gott?*

   _____

4. How many movements do Bach's cantatas usually have? _____

5. How many movements does Cantata No. 80 have?_____

6. In how many movements does Bach use the chorale tune? _____

   Which movements? _____

7. What is the structure of the first movement of this cantata?

   _____

   Can you easily hear the chorale tune in this setting? _____

8. What is the structure of the second movement, and where is the chorale

   tune heard? _____

   _____

9. What is the affection communicated by this movement? (Consider its

   text as well as music.) _____

*10. Compare the use of the chorale in the first and fifth movements.

   In which is it most prominently heard? _____

   _____

   _____

11. How do the trumpets and timpani contribute to the work? When were

   these parts added? _____

   _____

   _____

12. What was the religious occasion for this cantata?

_____

13. Were you familiar with the chorale tune *A Mightly Fortress Is Our God* before you heard this work? _____

If yes, where did you learn it? _____

About the Composer

14. What were Bach's three important positions, and what kind of music did he write in each?

1st period: _____

_____

2nd period: _____

_____

3rd period: _____

_____

15. What is his most important collection of keyboard works?

_____

16. In which sacred genres did Bach compose? _____

_____

17. In which instrumental genres did he compose? _____

_____

18. What accounts, in your opinion, for Bach's continued popularity today?

_____

_____

_____

30. *Reviewing* Baroque Instrumental Forms
(Chap. 24–26 C/Sh; 60–62 S)

Match the correct definitions on the right with the following instrumental forms.

_____ 1. solo concerto

a. a form based on a repeated bass line melody, or ground bass

_____ 2. concerto grosso

b. an organ work in which a traditional chorale tune is embellished

_____ 3. fugue

c. a short, continuous piece, often serves to introduce another movement

_____ 4. prelude

d. an orchestral introduction in two repeated sections: slow-fast

_____ 5. suite

e. a multimovement form based on the opposition of one player against a larger group

_____ 6. trio sonata

f. a form based on the opposition of a small and large group

_____ 7. chorale prelude

g. a series of dance movements, usually in the same key

_____ 8. passacaglia

h. a work for two violins or other melody instruments and basso continuo

_____ 9. French overture

i. an orchestral introduction in three sections: fast-slow-fast

_____ 10. Italian overture

j. a highly structured contrapuntal form, based on a single theme or subject

True or False

_____ 11. *The Four Seasons* is comprised of four concertos, each based on a poem describing a season of the year.

_____ 12. Vivaldi is known principally for his vocal music.

_____ 13. The Baroque concerto is most often based on an orchestral refrain, or ritornello procedure.

_____ 14. The standard Baroque concerto has three movements.

_____ 15. A chamber sonata is a suite of dances for full orchestra.

_____ 16. A suite is made up of dance movements in binary form.

_____ 17. The piano was the most popular Baroque keyboard instrument.

Mutiple Choice

_____ 18. The main theme of a fugue is known as the:
      a. episode.
      b. subject.
      c. fugato.

_____ 19. Passages in a fugal style within in a nonfugal piece are called:
      a. stretto.
      b. dominant.
      c. fugato.

_____ 20. The answer in a fugue is:
      a. the main theme imitated at another pitch level.
      b. the opening section.
      c. overlapping entries of the main theme.

_____ 21. A section of a fugue in which the main theme is not heard is called a(n):
      a. exposition.
      b. episode.
      c. recapitulation.

_____ 22. Which texture best defines a fugue?
      a. homophonic
      b. heterophonic
      c. polyphonic

_____ 23. The word "fugue" is from the Latin word for:
      a. flight.
      b. fight.
      c. fidget.

---

33. *Listening* Baroque Keyboard Music

* Bach: Chorale Prelude, *A Mighty Fortress Is Our God*
(Ein feste Burg ist unser Gott) (**LG** 23 C; 51 S)
Bach: Prelude and Fugue in C minor, from *The Well-Tempered Clavier,* Book 1
(**LG** 24 C; 13 Sh; 52 S)

---

*Listen to the Bach organ chorale prelude, and answer the following questions.

1. What is the origin of the tune on which Bach based this work?

   _____

   Is it easily recognizable throughout? _____

2. What musical techniques does Bach use to manipulate the tune?

   _____

3. How does an organ differ from a piano? _____

   _____

4. How does the organ achieve different timbres, or colors?

   _____

5. What role does the chorale prelude play in the Lutheran service?

   _____

Listen to the Bach Prelude and Fugue in C minor, and answer the following questions.

6. Bach's collection *The Well-Tempered Clavier* includes ____ books of

   keyboard works written for _____. Each book has

   _____ preludes and fugues, each in a different major or minor key.

   Thus there are a total of _____ preludes and fugues in the collection.

7. What is the main theme of the fugue called? _____

8. What is the first section of the fugue called, in which each voice is

   heard with the theme? _____

9. What is an episode? _____

   _____

   How many are in this fugue?_____

Match the following musical characteristics with either a or b.

       a. the prelude
       b. the fugue

____ 10. melodically oriented, with a theme that is heard repeatedly

____ 11. harmonically oriented, with chords establishing the motion

____ 12. a free, improvisational style

____ 13. a strict rhythmic pulse throughout

____ 14. form based on imitation

____ 15. linear movement with different "voices"

____ 16. ends on a C major chord

____ 17. homophonic texture

____ 18. polyphonic texture

19. Can you follow the form of the fugue from the line graph in the
Listening Guide? _____

20. What is highly structured about a fugue? _____

_____

_____

---

34. *Reviewing* From Baroque to Classical
(Trans. III C/Sh; Trans. IV S)

Complete the following questions.

1. What does the word "Rococo" mean? _____ *a shell* _____

2. What are the major characteristics of Rococo art?
   _____ *miniature, ornate* _____
   _____

   Name a well-known painter of the era. _____

3. Name two French composers that represent this style.
   _____ *Couperin + Rameau* _____

4. What traits were composers breaking away from in the Rococo?
   _____
   _____

5. What were the goals of the new "sensitive" style?
   _____

6. What major instrumental genres were developed during this era?
   _____

7. What was important about the premiere of *The Beggar's Opera* in 1728?
   _____ *death of traditional opera + birth* _____
   _____ *a time of popular songs + dances* _____

8. What were the circumstances that brought on the "War of the Buffoons"?
   _____
   _____
   _____

9. What changes did Gluck wish to bring about in opera seria?
   _____

10. What type of subjects did Gluck explore in his operas?
    _____

Comparing Baroque and Classical Styles

For each of the traits listed below, indicate with the appropriate letter the style to which it best relates.

  a. Baroque style
  b. Classical style

A 11. polyphonic textures

A 12. single affection for each work or movement

B 13. symmetrical and balanced phrases

A 14. use of terraced dynamics

B 15. improvisation limited to cadenzas

B 16. symphony and string quartet prevalent

A 17. organ and harpsichord as solo instruments

A 18. use of chromatic harmony for expression

B 19. piano as favored solo instrument

B 20. use of clarinet in orchestra

B 21. use of *crescendo* and *decrescendo*

22. Name the major composers of the Baroque era.

_____

Which of these did you know of prior to this course?

_____

23. Name the major composers of the Classical era.

_____

Which of these did you know of prior to this course?

_____

35. *Exploring* Crossover and the Growing Musical Audience
(**CP** 6 C/Sh; 14 S)

Fill in the answers below.

1. Describe how composers can merge actual traditional music with art music. _____

_____

_____

_____

2. How is traditional, or folk, music generally transmitted?

_____

_____

3. Why was John Gay's *Beggar's Opera* highly popular?

_____

_____

_____

_____

4. What is a ballad? *strophic songs with narrative texts*

_____

Name a ballad, if you can.

_____

5. What was the opera style developed in Germany as a response to ballad opera?_____

Name a masterwork in this genre.

_____

6. What modern American genre developed out of this tradition?

_____

7. Define the term "crossover." _____

_____

_____

Music listening assignment: Listen to selections from one of the works listed below (or another suggested by your instructor), which illustrate crossover to another style or genre. Describe what musical style the composer is known for and what style or styles are heard in this work.

Leonard Bernstein, *Mass*
Peter Townshend, *Tommy* (with the Who)
Paul McCartney, *Liverpool Oratorio*

_____

_____

_____

_____

_____

_____

_____

_____

_____

_____

_____

_____

_____

_____

_____

_____

_____

_____

_____

_____

_____

_____

_____

36. *Reviewing* Focus on Form
(Chap. 27–28 C/Sh; 36–37 S)

Fill in the answers below.

1. The smallest unit of a melody is called a(n) _motive_.

2. The principal melody in a composition is called a _theme_.

3. The manipulation and expansion of this melody is known as
   thematic development.

4. Name several techniques through which musical material is developed.

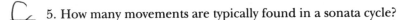

Multiple Choice

 5. How many movements are typically found in a sonata cycle?
   a. one   c. four
   b. two   d. six

_D_ 6. Which of the following genres is often in sonata cycle?
   a. string quartets   c. sonatas
   b. symphonies   d. all of the above

_B_ 7. Which of the following is the standard form for the first movement
   of a work in a sonata cycle?
   a. theme and variations form
   b. sonata-allegro form
   c. minuet and trio form
   d. binary (A-B) form

_B_ 8. Which are the three main sections of this first movement form?
   a. exposition-development-coda
   b. exposition-development-recapitulation
   c. minuet-trio-minuet
   d. theme–variation 1–variation 2

 9. The section of a form that serves as a transition, often to another
   key center, is known as a:
   a. codetta.   c. bridge.
   b. theme group.   d. development.

_D_ 10. The final section of a movement that rounds off the piece,
   establishing the tonic key, is called the:
   a. bridge.   c. introduction.
   b. development.   d. coda.

_a_ 11. What is the standard tempo scheme of a sonata cycle?
      a. fast-moderate-slow-fast
      b. slow-fast-moderate-fast
      c. fast-slow-moderate-fast
      d. fast-slow-fast-slow

12. Describe how the two principal themes of a sonata-allegro form differ from each other.

Theme (or theme group) 1   Theme (or theme group) 2

_____

_____

13. How does the final section or restatement of the above themes differ from what is heard in the exposition?

_____

_____

14. What is the purpose of the development section?

_____

_____

15. What elements can be varied in a theme and variations form?

_____

_____

True or False

_F_ 16. Minuet and trio form is most often found as the fourth movement of a sonata cycle.

_T_ 17. The minuet and trio form grew out of earlier dance forms.

_F_ 18. A minuet and trio is generally in duple meter.

_T_ 19. One type of rondo form can be outlined as **A-B-A-C-A-B-A**.

_F_ 20. A rondo features one main idea that keeps coming back throughout the work.

_F_ 21. A coda provides an introduction to a movement.

_T_ 22. Rounded binary form brings back the first theme at the close of the second section.

---

37. *Reviewing* **The Classical Spirit**
(Chap. 29–30 C/Sh; 38–39 S)

Fill in the answers below.

1. List general attributes of the Classical style that parallel those listed for the Romantic:

   Classical   Romantic

   a. _____   a. longing for strangeness,
      _____   ecstasy, and wonder

   b. _____   b. intense subjectivity

   c. _____   c. symbolized by Dionysus, God
      _____   of passion and intoxication

   d. _____   d. uninhibited emotional
                                                 expression

Choose the best answer for each.

____ 2. Which historical event took place first?
         a. French Revolution
         b. American Revolution

____ 3. Which culture was idealized in the eighteenth century?
         a. the Medieval world
         b. the world of ancient Greece and Rome

____ 4. Which eighteenth-century movement helped shape the modern world?
         a. the Protestant Reformation
         b. the Industrial Revolution

Match the following Classical-era figures with the correct description.

  E   5. Friedrich von Schiller   a. French revolutionary painter

  C   6. Thomas Jefferson   b. enlightened czarina of Russia

  A   7. Jacques Louis David   c. principal author of the Declaration
                                        of Independence

  B   8. Catherine the Great   d. English experimenter who invented
                                        the cotton gin

  D   9. Eli Whitney   e. German early Romantic poet

10. Who are the four musical masters of the Viennese school?

    a. _____   b. _____

    c. _____   d. _____

11. Check those characteristics below that properly describe the Classical musical style (one check per pair of letters).

_____ a. disjunct, wide-ranging melodies or

_____ b. simple, singable melodies

_____ c. regular, symmetrical phrasing with clear cadences or

_____ d. irregular, asymmetrical phrasing with weak or covered cadences

_____ e. chromatic harmony or

_____ f. diatonic harmony

_____ g. free, programmatic forms or

_____ h. large-scale, absolute forms

_____ i. incorporation of folk songs and dances or

_____ j. incorporation of non-Western melodies

_____ k. weak or free meters or

_____ l. strong, regular meters

12. How would you describe the patronage system? What were the advantages and disadvantages to artists serving under this system?

_____

_____

_____

_____

_____

13. What role did women play in music during this era?

_____

_____

_____

_____

---

38. *Exploring* Concert Life in America: Then and Now
(CP 7 C/Sh; 6 S)

Complete the following questions.

1. What composers were the most frequently heard in American concerts of the eighteenth century? _____

   _____

2. Describe some aspects of eighteenth-century American concerts:

   _____

   _____

   _____

   _____

3. How did opera performances differ from those today?

   _____

   _____

   _____

4. What is the literal meaning of the word "encore"? _____
   What does it mean when the audience asks for an encore?

   _____

5. Which famous American statesmen were amateur musicians?

   _____

6. What were considered desirable musical abilities for eighteenth-century women? _____

   _____

7. Name several major music organizations that first appeared in the nineteenth century. _____

   _____

Library assignment: Select A or B below.

A. Go to the microfilm section of your college (or community) library. Investigate whether they have any eighteenth- or nineteenth-century newspapers on film there (for example, the *New York Times* or the *Boston Globe*). If available, select a film from this era at random, put it on the machine (following the directions for threading the film), and scroll through until you find an announcement of an upcoming concert. Fill in the information below.

B. Locate a concert announcement in the calendar section of a current newspaper. Note the following information.

Title of newspaper: _____

Date of issue: _____

Section and page of announcement: _____

Concert information (date, time, price, location): _____

_____

_____

_____

List the works and composers to be performed.

_____

_____

_____

_____

_____

_____

_____

_____

_____

Comments: _____

_____

_____

_____

_____

> **39.** *Reviewing* **Chamber Music and Symphony in the Classical Era**
> (Chap. 31–33 C/Sh; 40–42 S)

Answer the following questions.

1. What is chamber music? *for small ensembles* _____

2. What was the favored chamber ensemble in the Classical era, and what
   is its makeup? _____

   _____

3. Name several other common chamber ensembles. _____

   _____

4. List several forms of popular entertainment music during the era.

   _____

Match the following forms on the right to the string quartet movement
where they would most likely appear:

____ 5. First movement   a. theme and variations form

____ 6. Second movement   b. rondo form

____ 7. Third movement   c. sonata-allegro form

____ 8. Fourth movement   d. minuet and trio form

Match the following string quartet traits with the composer on the right best
associated with each.

_B_ 9. use of folk elements   a. Mozart

_C_ 10. scherzo replaced minuet   b. Haydn

_C_ 11. motivic development   c. Beethoven

_A_ 12. lyrical, elegant themes

The Symphony

13. From which earlier form did the symphony evolve? _____

14. What contributions did Mannheim musicians make to the symphony?

   _____

15. Approximately how many players made up a Classical-era orchestra?

   _____ Which instrument families are represented?

   _____

16. In what type of setting were symphonies performed in the eighteenth century? _____

    In what setting are they performed today? _____

17. Which movement of the symphony is generally the longest and the most complex? _____

    What is its form? _____

18. Which movement is generally the fastest? _____

    What are typical forms for this movement?

    _____

19. Which movement is based on a dance form? _____

    What is the character of this dance movement?_____

    _____

20. Which movement is generally the slowest? _____

    What forms are typical for it?

    _____

21. Which movement is probably the most lyrical? _____

22. What does the term "monothematic" mean in relation to the symphony?

    _____

    Which composer is associated with this form?

    _____

40. *Listening* Eighteenth-Century Chamber Music
*Haydn: String Quartet in D minor, Op. 76, No. 2 (*Quinten*), (**LG** 26 C; 19 S)
Mozart: *Eine kleine Nachtmusik,* K. 525 (**LG** 27 C; 14 Sh; 20 S)

*Listen to the last movement of Haydn's Quartet, Op. 76, No. 2, and answer the following questions.

1. How many string quartets did Haydn write? _____

2. When were his Opus 76 quartets written? _____

3. In which key is Op. 76, No. 2, written? _____

4. How many movements does this quartet have? _____

5. Give the general tempo and form for each movement below.

   I. _____

   II. _____

   III. _____

   IV. _____

6. What is the nickname for this quartet? _____

   Why is it called this? _____

   _____

7. What elements make the fourth movement sound dancelike?

   _____

   _____

8. How does Haydn provide musical contrast in this work?

   _____

   _____

Listen to Mozart's *Eine kleine Nachtmusik,* and answer the following questions.

9. What does the title *Eine kleine Nachtmusik* mean literally?

   _____ A little night music _____

10. Is this work __✓__ a string quartet or _____ a serenade?

    What size ensemble was it written for? _____

11. List the general tempo and form for each movement.

 I. _____

 II. _____

 III. _____

 IV. _____

12. In what key is the work? _____

 Which movement is not in this key? _____

*13. How would you describe the themes in the first movement?

 Theme 1: _____

 Theme 2: _____

14. How would you describe the themes in the third movement?

 Minuet: _____

 Trio: _____

 Which section sounds more dancelike? _____

15. How does Mozart create contrast with the two themes of the last

 movement? _____

 _____

16. What kind of concert setting was this written for?

 _____

 _____

17. Do you find chamber music a listening challenge? _____

 Explain your answer. _____

 _____

 _____

---

41. *Listening* **Eighteenth-Century Symphony**

*Mozart: Symphony No. 40 in G minor, First Movement (**LG** 28 C; 21 S)
Haydn: Symphony No. 100, in G major (*Military*), Second Movement
(**LG** 29 C; 15 Sh; 22 S)
Beethoven: Symphony No. 5 in C minor, Op. 67 (**LG** 30 C; 16 Sh; 23 S)

---

*Listen to Mozart's Symphony No. 40 in G minor, and answer the questions below.

1. What is the overall form of this symphony (movements and tempo)?

2. What kind of motive provides the building block for the first theme?

3. What techniques does Mozart use to vary material in the development section of the first movement?

4. Unlike many Classical-era symphonies, Mozart's Symphony No. 40 is in the minor mode. What effect is produced by this choice of harmony?

5. Why do you think this symphony was called the *Romantic* by the Viennese?

6. Compare Haydn's Symphony No. 100 and Beethoven's Symphony No. 5, then complete the following chart.

	Symphony No. 100	Symphony No. 5
a. First movement		
Tempo:		
Form:		
b. Second movement		
Tempo:		
Form:		

81

c. Third movement

    Tempo: _____

    Form: _____

d. Fourth movement

    Tempo: _____

    Form: _____

7. Do both symphonies follow the standard sonata-cycle plan? _____

8. How does Haydn evoke a military character in the second movement of his symphony? _____

_____

9. What new orchestral instruments are heard in this work?

_____

10. What makes the first movement of Beethoven's Symphony No. 5 so memorable? _____

_____

11. What traits of the Beethoven symphony sound Romantic?

_____

_____

---

42. *Exploring* East Meets West: Turkish Influences on the Viennese Classics (CP 8 C/Sh; 7 S)

Answer the following questions.

1. To which empire did eighteenth-century Austria belong?

   _____

   To which empire did Turkey belong? _____

2. What is a Janissary band? *mounted military bands*

   _____

   When and where did it originate?

   _____

3. How did Western Europeans come to know the sound of the Janissary

   ensemble? _____

   _____

4. What instruments were added to this band in the seventeenth century?

   _____

   _____

5. Which Classical composers tried to imitate the Janissary band in their

   music? _____

6. What permanent contribution did this ensemble make to the Western

   orchestra? _____

   _____

7. What other Western music group did the Janissary ensemble influence?

   _____

8. Which Islamic religious ceremony did Beethoven attempt to imitate in

   The Ruins of Athens? _____

   Describe this ceremony. _____

   _____

   _____

Music listening assignment: Locate a recording of Turkish music in your library (or ask your instructor to provide one from the Music Example Bank). Listen to it, and describe the musical style and instruments in your own words. Note what sounds foreign about it and what sounds familiar.

_____

_____

_____

_____

_____

_____

_____

_____

_____

_____

_____

_____

_____

_____

_____

_____

_____

_____

_____

_____

_____

_____

_____

_____

_____

_____

---

43. *Reviewing* **The Classical Masters**
(Chap. 32, 34–35 C/Sh; 41, 43–44 S)

Choose the composer who best fits the description below.

    a. Joseph Haydn
    b. Wolfgang Amadeus Mozart
    c. Ludwig van Beethoven

_B_ 1. The composer who was a child prodigy as a composer and performer.

_C_ 2. The composer who grew deaf at the height of his compositional career.

_____ 3. The composer generally known as the "father of the symphony."

_B_ 4. The composer who died young, while writing a requiem mass.

_A_ 5. The composer who thrived for many years under the patronage system.

_A_ 6. The composer of the *London* symphonies.

_C_ 7. The composer of thirty-two piano sonatas, including the *Moonlight*.

_B_ 8. The composer who is well-known for opera buffa.

_C_ 9. The composer whose last symphony includes a choral setting of Schiller's *Ode to Joy.*

_C_ 10. The composer who spanned the transition between the Classical and Romantic eras.

11. List for comparison the number of symphonies written by each composer below:
    Haydn _100_   Mozart _40_   Beethoven _9_

12. Why did Mozart write fewer symphonies than Haydn?

_____

_____

13. Why did Beethoven write fewer symphonies than Haydn or Mozart?

_____

_____

14. What European country can be associated with the lives of all three of these musicians? _____

Multiple Choice

___ 15. The K. number following each Mozart work refers to:
    a. the name of the man who catalogued his compositions.
    b. the key or tonality of the composition.

___ 16. Which Mozart opera was written in German and was popular in the Viennese theater?
    a. *The Magic Flute*
    b. *The Clemency of Titus*

___ 17. Haydn worked for many years for:
    a. the Prince-Archbishop of Salzburg.
    b. the Hungarian noble family of Esterházy.

___ 18. Which was a popular oratorio by Haydn?
    a. *The Creation*
    b. *Messiah*

___ 19. Which composer wrote only one opera, *Fidelio?*
    a. Joseph Haydn
    b. Ludwig van Beethoven

___ 20. Late in his life, Haydn made several visits to _____, where he was commissioned to write a group of symphonies.
    a. Italy
    b. England

___ 21. The composer of the *Eroica* Symphony was:
    a. Beethoven.
    b. Mozart.

22. How do you account for the continued popularity of these three Classical composers?

_____

_____

_____

_____

_____

---

45. *Reviewing* The Concerto and Sonata in the Classical Era
(Chap. 36–37 C/Sh; 45–46 S)

Multiple Choice

b 1. How many movements are standard in a concerto?
- a. two
- b. three
- c. four
- d. five or more

c 2. How many movements are standard in a sonata?
- a. one or two
- b. two or three
- c. three or four
- d. five or more

c 3. Which tempo scheme is standard for the concerto?
- a. slow-fast
- b. fast-slow-fast-faster
- c. fast-slow-fast
- d. slow-moderate-fast

4. What is a cadenza, and when is it generally played? _____

_____

_____

5. What two forms does the first movement of a concerto adapt?

_____

6. What were the favored solo instruments in the Classical concerto?

_____

7. What instrument(s) did Mozart play?

_____

8. For whom did he write his Piano Concerto in G major, K. 453?

_____

9. What were the favored instruments in the Classical sonata?

_____

10. What is a duo sonata? _____

_____

Match the following virtuoso women performers with the correct description.

      a. Barbara von Ployer   c. Maria Anna Mozart
      b. Maddalena Lombardini   d. Maria Theresa von Paradis

_____ 11. An accomplished pianist who was Mozart's sister.

_____ 12. A gifted piano student of Mozart's, for whom he wrote two concertos.

_____ 13. A talented blind pianist and organist, for whom both Mozart and Salieri wrote concertos.

_____ 14. A virtuoso violinst who was a student of Tartini and also a composer of violin concertos.

15. Choose two of the women above, and describe how each excelled as a musician.

_____

_____

_____

_____

_____

_____

_____

---

48. *Listening* Mozart's *Marriage of Figaro*
(**LG** 35 C; 19 Sh; 28 S)

Listen to the selection on your recording from *The Marriage of Figaro.*

1. What type of opera is this? _____

2. What are some of the typical characteristics of this opera type?

_____

_____

3. How does this opera differ from opera seria? _____

_____

_____

4. Who was the librettist for *The Marriage of Figaro?*

_____

5. Name other Mozart operas by the same librettist.

_____

6. What was the literary basis for *The Marriage of Figaro?*

_____

7. In what ways does this opera satirize the aristocracy?

_____

_____

8. What is a trouser role? _____

_____

9. What is your reaction to the trouser role in *The Marriage of Figaro?*

_____

10. What do you learn about the character of Cherubino from his aria

(No. 6)? _____

11. What purpose is served by the long recitative between Cherubino's aria
(No. 6) and the trio (No. 7) in *The Marriage of Figaro?*

_____

_____

_____

12. Consider the three characters singing in the trio (No. 7), and suggest below what emotion each is expressing and how the music helps communicate this emotion.

The Count: _____

_____

Basilio: _____

_____

Susanna: _____

_____

13. What aspects of the plot of *The Marriage of Figaro* strike you as unrealistic or far-fetched?

_____

_____

_____

14. In what ways would this story be changed in a modern-day update?

_____

_____

_____

**49. *Reviewing* Mendelssohn and the Transition from Classicism
to Romanticism** (Trans. IV C/Sh; Trans. II S)

Answer the following questions.

1. Which two early Romantic composers can be viewed as direct heirs of
   the Classical tradition?

2. How did Felix Mendelssohn make his living in music?

3. How did he contribute to the revival of interest in Baroque music?

4. Name several of Mendelssohn's best-known compositions.

5. For what musical activities was Fanny Mendelssohn noted?

*Listen to the Overture from *A Midsummer Night's Dream,* and answer the
following.

6. What is the basis for the program (or story) for this work?

7. Describe how Mendelssohn's music evokes the images of fairies, lovers,
   and clowns.

8. What Classical form does this Overture suggest? _____
   Describe its main sections. _____

Comparing Classical and Romantic Styles

For each of the following musical traits, indicate whether it is best associated with the Classical or Romantic style.

      a. Classical style
      b. Romantic style

_____ 9. interest in the bizarre and morbid

_____ 10. diatonic harmony predominant

_____ 11. unusual ranges on instruments

_____ 12. one-movement programmatic forms

_____ 13. dance rhythms with regular beats and accents

_____ 14. rise of middle-class audience

_____ 15. freer rhythms and tempo rubato

_____ 16. emotional restraint

_____ 17. symmetrical, balanced phrases

_____ 18. wide-ranging dynamic contrasts

_____ 19. introduction of the English horn and tuba

_____ 20. preference for absolute forms

_____ 21. sonata-allegro form established

_____ 22. aristocratic audiences

_____ 23. much expanded melodic and harmonic chromaticism

24. What dates are generally assigned to the Classical period?

_____ to the Romantic period? _____

25. Describe how Beethoven (or Schubert or Mendelssohn) can be viewed as transitional composers between these two eras.

_____

_____

_____

_____

_____

_____

50. *Reviewing* The Romantic Movement
(Chap. 40–41 C; 39–40 Sh; 11–12 S)

Answer the following.

1. What were the ideals of the early Romantic movement?

_____

_____

2. What social changes resulted from the French Revolution?

_____

_____

_____

3. What was the slogan of the revolution? _____

Match the following Romantic figures with the descriptions on the right.

_____ 4. Heinrich Heine   a. English novelist

_____ 5. Victor Hugo   b. French painter

_____ 6. Eugène Delacroix   c. German poet

_____ 7. Lord Byron   d. English poet

_____ 8. Emily Brontë   e. French novelist

9. What effect did the Industrial Revolution have on the production of

musical instruments? _____

_____

_____

_____

10. What new instruments were developed in the Romantic era?

_____

_____

_____

11. What was the effect of the era on educational opportunities in music?

_____

_____

12. What is meant by "exoticism" in music? _____

_____

_____

13. Name a musical work that is representative of exoticism.

Composer: _____ Title: _____

Multiple Choice

_____ 14. Which of the following is <u>not</u> typical of Romantic music?
   a. lyrical, singable melodies
   b. expanded forms
   c. smaller orchestras
   d. increased dissonance for expression

_____ 15. Which role did Romantic composers generally <u>not</u> fill?
   a. educators
   b. servants to the aristocracy
   c. performing artists
   d. conductors

Complete the following questions.

16. Who were the musical "stars" in the nineteenth century?

_____

_____

17. What roles in music did women fill in the Romantic era?

_____

_____

18. What educational advantages in music were open to women?

_____

_____

19. What prejudices did women musicians, artists, and writers have to
    contend with in the nineteenth century?

_____

_____

_____

_____

_____

> **51. *Reviewing* Nineteenth-Century Art Song**
> (Chap. 42–44 C; 41–42 Sh; 13–15 S)

Complete the following questions.

1. A song form in which the same melody is repeated for each stanza, often heard in popular music, is known as _____.

2. A song form that is composed from beginning to end without repetitions of whole sections is called _____.

3. A song type that features some repetition or variations of a melody and new material is known as _____.

4. A group of Lieder unified by a descriptive or narrative theme is known as a _____. Name one and its composer.

_____

True or False

_____ 5. A Lied is a German art song for solo voice and piano.

_____ 6. Folk elements are sometimes incorporated into the Lied.

_____ 7. The composer normally writes the lyrics for the Lied.

_____ 8. The Lied composer often attempts to portray musically the imagery of the poem.

_____ 9. The favorite themes of the Lied include love and nature.

_____ 10. The piano was dying in popularity at the time of the Romantic Lied.

11. Name one important German poet whose texts were frequently set to music; cite one specific work and its composer.

Poet   Poem   Composer

_____   _____   _____

12. Name two additional important composers of Lieder.

a. _____

b. _____

Schubert and the Lied

13. When was Schubert's *Erlking* written? _____

    How old was the composer when he wrote it?_____

    Who wrote the poem for this song? _____

14. What is Schubert's *Winter's Journey*? _____

    Who was the poet for this work? _____

15. Approximately how many songs did Schubert write in his lifetime?

    _____

*16. What is a "Schubertiad"? _____

    _____

*Brahms as a Lied Composer

17. What composers took Brahms into their home in his youth?

    _____

18. What themes do Brahms's Lieder express? _____

    _____

19. Approximately how many songs did Brahms write? _____

20. How do Brahms's songs reflect his nationalism?

    _____

    _____

52. *Exploring* Folk Song and the Lied
(**CP** 10 C/Sh; 1 S)

Complete the following questions.

1. What distinguishes art music from traditional music? _____

_____

_____

_____

2. What are the basic musical elements of German folk song style?
   (Consider melody, rhythm/meter, form, and text setting.)

_____

_____

_____

Name a German folk song with these characteristics.

_____

3. What is the popular name of Brahms's *Wiegenlied?*

_____

4. From where does the text for this Brahms song come?

_____

5. What Austrian dance does the rhythm of *Wiegenlied* follow?

_____

6. Why are there small variants in the way different people learn the
   melodies and texts of folk songs? _____

_____

_____

7. Why do composers imitate their native traditional music in their art
   music? _____

_____

_____

Musical exercise. Select a folk song (or children's song) for which you know the melody and words. Sing it to yourself several times, and then answer the questions below.

Name of song: _____

Write its text as a poem (one strophe).

_____

_____

_____

_____

_____

Country of origin (if known): _____

Melody (shape, range, conjunct or disjunct): _____

_____

Rhythm/meter (use of upbeat at beginning, duple, triple, compound

meter): _____

Form (strophic, use of refrain): _____

Text setting (syllabic, neumatic, melismatic): _____

_____

Do you know any variants for this song (text or music)?_____

If yes, describe. _____

_____

How and when did you learn this song?_____

_____

How widely known is it, and what function does it serve? _____

_____

_____

_____

> ### 53. *Listening* Romantic Lieder
> Schubert: *Erlking* (**LG** 37 C; 20 Sh; 2 S)
> *Brahms: *Futile Serenade* (**LG** 38 C; 3 S)

Listen to Schubert's *Erlking* while following the Listening Guide, and answer the questions below.

1. How does the piano establish the mood of Schubert's *Erlking* at the

   beginning? _____

   _____

2. What is the form of this song? _____

   Is any music or idea repeated? _____

3. Describe how Schubert portrays each of the four characters in the song musically with only one singer.

   Narrator: _____

   _____

   Father: _____

   _____

   Son: _____

   _____

   Erlking: _____

   _____

4. How does Schubert use dissonance for dramatic effect?

   _____

5. Bearing in mind the drama of Schubert's *Erlking*, suggest a story (either from literature or from a movie) that you think would make a successful Lied, with solo voice and piano. Briefly describe the story, and suggest some effects that might be achieved in the Lied.

   _____

   _____

   _____

   _____

   _____

   _____

*Listen to the Brahms song *Futile Serenade* while following the Listening Guide. Answer the questions below.

6. What type of variation occurs to make this song a modified strophic

   form? _____

7. How would you describe the overall mood of this Lied?

   _____

8. What characteristics contribute to the folklike nature of this song?

   _____

   What qualities make it sound dancelike? _____

   _____

9. How would you describe the role of the piano in this Lied?

   _____

   _____

10. This Lied illustrates a timeless theme: boy wants girl, but girl refuses
    boy. Name a more recent popular song that has a similar theme. How
    does its text and music differ from Brahms's song? How is it similar?

    _____

    _____

    _____

    _____

    _____

    _____

    _____

---

54. *Reviewing* The Nineteenth-Century Piano Piece and Its Composers (Chap. 46–48 C; 44–45 Sh; 17–19 S)

True or False

_____ 1. The piano became a popular instrument for amateur musicians.

_____ 2. The piano changed little technically during the nineteenth century.

_____ 3. The nineteenth century was an age of great virtuoso pianists.

4. Which nineteenth-century composers contributed to modern piano technique? _____

5. What are some of the descriptive titles that Romantic composers gave to their piano works? _____

_____

6. Why is Chopin called the "poet of the piano"?

_____

_____

7. What was Chopin's national heritage? _____

8. What is tempo rubato? _____

_____

9. With which famous woman writer was Chopin romantically involved?

_____

10. What are some of the types of small forms of piano music that Chopin wrote? _____

In which large forms did he write? _____

Of these forms, which can be viewed as nationalistic?

_____

11. What music did Chopin write that did <u>not</u> include piano?

_____

*12. In which country was Franz Liszt born? _____

*13. With which famous writer was Liszt romantically involved?

_____

*14. What other aristocratic woman was important in Liszt's life?

_____

*15. What life-style did Liszt choose in his later years?

_____

*16. Liszt devised a technique of developing a theme through constant variation of its melody, rhythm, or harmony. This process is known as

_____.

*17. Which composer did Liszt describe as writing the "music of the future"?

_____

18. Describe Clara Schumann's early musical training.

_____

19. What types of compositions did Clara Schumann write?

_____

20. What was her relationship with Robert Schumann? _____

    with Brahms? _____

21. What was the public reaction to Clara Schumann as a pianist?

_____

22. What difficulties did a woman composer have in the nineteenth century?

_____

_____

_____

_____

---

55. *Listening* Romantic Piano Music

Chopin: Polonaise in A flat, Op. 53 (**LG** 39 C; 21 Sh; 4 S)
*Chopin: Prelude in E minor, Op. 28, No. 4 (**LG** 40 C; 5 S)
*Liszt:: *Wild Hunt (Wilde Jagd)*, Transcendental Etude No. 8 (**LG** 41 C; 6 S)
Clara Schumann: Scherzo, Op. 10 (**LG** 42 C; 22 Sh; 7 S)

Listen to Chopin's Polonaise in A flat, and answer the following.

1. What sounds nationalistic about this work? _____

   _____

2. Describe the character of the main theme (after the introduction).

   _____

3. Describe the mood of the contrasting middle section (**B**) of the work.

   _____

4. Do you recognize the return of the opening theme? _____

5. Does the performance you heard use tempo rubato? _____

   Where in the piece? _____

*Listen to Chopin's Prelude in E minor, and answer the following.

6. This prelude is a:

   ____ a. large-scale, multisectional work for piano or

   ____ b. small character work for piano.

7. The opening phrase of this prelude is:

   ____ a. disjunct with a wide range or

   ____ b. conjunct with a narrow range.

8. The work is performed:

   ____ a. with some freedom, or rubato, in the rhythm or

   ____ b. with strict tempo and rhythm.

9. The meter is:

   ____ a. strong and dancelike in this piece or

   ____ b. gentle and veiled in this piece.

10. How would you characterize the mood of this work?

    _____

11. Do you think this prelude is difficult to perform well? _____
    Explain. _____

*Listen to Liszt's étude *Wild Hunt,* and answer the following.

12. From which collection is *Wild Hunt?* _____
    What is the purpose of these works? _____
    _____

13. How do you think Liszt evokes a hunting theme in this work?
    _____

14. For what other types of compositions is Liszt known?
    _____

15. Does this work seem to be virtuosic to play? _____
    Explain. _____

Listen to Clara Schumann's Scherzo, Op. 10, and answer the following.

16. Describe the character of each section of this work.
    Scherzo theme: _____
    Trio 1: _____
    Trio 2: _____

17. Does the marking *con passione* (with passion) seem appropriate? _____
    Explain. _____
    _____

18. What are some of the features that make this a display work?
    _____
    _____

19. Is there anything about this work that seems "feminine" in your
    opinion? _____ Explain. _____
    _____

---

56. *Exploring* **Polish Folk Dance and Music**
(**CP** 11 C/Sh; 2 S)

Complete the following questions.

1. What was Chopin's cultural heritage? _____

    _____

2. Describe the polonaise as a dance. _____

    _____

    _____

3. What other Polish dance types did Chopin imitate in his piano music?

    _____

    Describe these dances. _____

    _____

    _____

4. What is the origin of the word "polka"? _____

    _____

5. What are the musical characteristics of the polka? _____

    _____

    What kind of instruments traditionally accompanied the dance?

    _____

6. Describe the popularity of the polka in the nineteenth century.

    _____

    _____

    _____

7. What regions of the United States have large settlements of Polish-

    Americans? _____

    _____

    _____

Music listening assignment: Select A or B below.

A. Locate a recording of a polka performed by a modern polka band (or hear a live performance of one). Describe the work's characteristics below.

B. Locate a recording of a polka set by one of the following composers. Describe its characteristics below.

   Johann Strauss
   Bedřich Smetana
   Igor Stravinsky (*Circus Polka*)

Selection: _____

Group/Composer: _____

Instruments used: _____

_____

_____

Melodic and rhythmic characteristics: _____

_____

_____

_____

Tempo and meter: _____

Harmony and texture: _____

_____

_____

Describe other elements that make this work sound dancelike.

_____

_____

_____

Comments: _____

_____

_____

57. *Reviewing* Romantic Program Music and Nationalism
(Chap. 49–51 C; 46–48 Sh; 20–22 S)

Match the following terms with their definitions below:

    a. absolute music   d. program music
    b. concert overture   e. incidental music
    c. program symphony   f. symphonic poem

_____ 1. instrumental music that has some literary or pictorial association supplied by the composer

_____ 2. music lacking any literary or pictorial association

_____ 3. a type of program music written to accompany plays

_____ 4. a one-movement work for orchestra with a literary program

_____ 5. a multimovement orchestral work with literary program

_____ 6. a one-movement work originally written to introduce a larger work, but played independently

Multiple Choice

_____ 7. What composer is generally credited with the first use of the term "symphonic poem"?
    a. Franz Liszt
    b. Hector Berlioz
    c. Felix Mendelssohn

_____ 8. The chief difference between a symphonic poem and a program symphony is:
    a. the nature of the program.
    b. the number of movements in the work.
    c. the number of musicians involved.

*9. What example did we study of incidental music?

_____

What was its program? _____

10. What example did we study of a program symphony? _____

_____

11. In what ways do composers express their nationalism through music?

_____

_____

Match the following composers with the correct national school.

a. Russian school   d. English school
b. Czech school   e. Spanish school
c. Scandinavian school

____ 12. Jean Sibelius   ___ 16. Edvard Grieg

____ 13. Bedřich Smetana   ___ 17. Alexander Borodin

____ 14. Manuel de Falla   ___ 18. Edward Elgar

____ 15. Mily Balakirev   ___ 19. Nikolai Rimsky-Korsakov

20. The term "program music" can apply to music for film and television as well as to nineteenth-century instrumental music. Describe briefly a movie or television production you have seen recently and tell how the music helped to portray the story or establish the mood.

Program: _____

_____

_____

Musical description: _____

_____

_____

_____

58. *Listening* Berlioz and Musorgsky
Berlioz: *Symphonie fantastique*, Fifth Movement (**LG** 43 C; 23 Sh; 8 S)
Musorgsky: *Pictures at an Exhibition*, excerpts (**LG** 44 C'; 24 Sh; 9 S)

Listen to Berlioz's *Symphonie fantastique*, and answer the following.

1. When and where did Berlioz write the *Symphonie fantastique?*

2. What is "Romantic" about this work and its program?

3. Who was the inspiration behind this work?

4. What is an *idée fixe?*

5. How does Berlioz use this technique to unify his symphony?

6. What effect does the use of the *Dies irae* chant have?

7. What techniques does Berlioz use to depict the story in this movement?

8. What is your reaction to the story behind this musical work?

Listen to the selections from Musorgsky's *Pictures at an Exhibition,* and answer the following.

9. What is the basis for the program of *Pictures at an Exhibition?*

_____

10. For what medium was it originally written? _____

11. When was it arranged for orchestra? _____

    By whom? _____

*12. Describe the character of the *Promenade* theme. _____

_____

13. What are the subjects of some of the inner movements?

_____

_____

*14. What is the basis for the ninth movement, *The Hut on Fowl's Legs?*

_____

*15. What musical characteristics portray the wild ride of Baba-Yaga?

_____

16. What is the basis for *The Great Gate of Kiev?* _____

_____

17. What makes this movement sound majestic? _____

_____

18. What is the form of this movement? _____

19. At what point is the *Promenade* theme heard in the last movement?

_____

20. For what movie or TV scene would you find this movement appropriate background music? _____

_____

_____

_____

59. *Exploring* Folk Tales Set to Music
(**CP** 12 C/Sh; 3 S)

Complete the following questions.

1. What lessons do folk tales teach? _____

_____

_____

2. Cite a folk tale you know and its moral or lesson.

_____

_____

_____

_____

3. Who is the Russian folk figure Baba-Yaga? _____

_____

_____

_____

4. From which folk collection does the tale of "Hansel and Gretel" come?

_____

5. What is the source of the tale of "Aladdin"? _____

_____

   of "Sleeping Beauty" and "Cinderella"? _____

_____

   of "The Little Mermaid"? _____

6. What is the folk basis for Tchaikovsky's ballet *The Nutcracker?*

_____

_____

7. What musical genres lend themselves to settings of folk tales?

_____

Music listening assignment: Listen to one of the musical works below, which sets a folk tale. Familiarize yourself with the story (find the original tale or read over the recording notes), and describe below how the music portrays the events of the story.

Maurice Ravel,   *Mother Goose Suite* (*Ma mère l'oye*) (French tales by Perrault, first two movements only, orchestral version)
>   "Pavane de la Belle au bois dormant" ("Sleeping Beauty")
>   "Petit Poucet" ("Tom Thumb")

Sergei Prokofiev, *Cinderella* (ballet suite after Perrault tale)
P. Tchaikovsky,   *The Sleeping Beauty*, Op. 66a (ballet suite after Perrault tale)
Richard Strauss,   *Till Eulenspiegel's Merry Pranks* (German tale)
Sergei Prokofiev, *Peter and the Wolf* (modern Russian tale)

_____
_____
_____
_____
_____
_____
_____
_____
_____
_____
_____
_____
_____
_____
_____
_____
_____
_____
_____
_____
_____
_____

---

60. *Reviewing* Absolute Forms: The Symphony and the Concerto
(Chap. 52, 54 C; 49–50 Sh; 25 S)

Terms to Remember

absolute music   scherzo
cadenza   sonata-allegro form
concerto   symphony
motive   theme
                                  tutti

Complete the following questions.

1. The symphony is a large-scale work for orchestra, made up of several

   independent parts, or _____.

2. The symphony first became an important form in the _____

   era.

3. The three Viennese composers who mastered the form and handed it

   down to Romantic composers were _____,

   _____, and _____.

4. The symphony cycle most typically has _____ movements.

5. Of these, the _____ movement is usually the most highly

   structured, and features the use of _____ form.

6. What forms are typical for the second movement of a symphony?

   _____

Multiple Choice

____ 7. Which is the most typical tempo structure for a symphony?
         a. fast, moderate triple dance, slow, fast
         b. slow, fast, fast, moderate triple dance
         c. fast, slow, moderate triple dance, fast

____ 8. The third movement of the nineteenth-century symphony is most
         likely in:
         a. scherzo form.
         b. sonata-allegro form.
         c. theme and variations form.

____ 9. The concerto most typically has:
         a. one movement.
         b. three movements.
         c. four movements.

119

10. In what ways did nineteenth-century composers change the overall form of the symphony? _____

_____

11. How does the form of the first movement of a concerto differ from sonata-allegro form in a symphony? _____

_____

_____

12. Who were some of the major contributors to the Romantic concerto?

_____

13. How do you account for the rise in virtuosity in the nineteenth century?

_____

_____

14. Since absolute forms such as the symphony and the concerto generally have no program, what gives them their sense of shape and meaning?

_____

_____

_____

---

61. *Listening* **Brahms and Dvořák as Symphonists***
*Brahms, Symphony No. 4 in E minor, Fourth Movement (**LG** 45 C; 10 S)
*Dvořák, Symphony No. 9 in E minor, *From the New World*, Second Movement
  (**LG** 46 C; 11 S)

---

*Listen to the fourth movement of Symphony No. 4 by Brahms, and answer
the following.

_____ 1. Which of the following is <u>not</u> true of this movement's form?
  a. It is borrowed from the Baroque passacaglia.
  b. It has an overall structure of **A-B-A.**
  c. It is in duple meter, with the melody remaining in the bass
     throughout.

_____ 2. Which best describes this Brahms symphony?
  a. a program symphony based on a literary subject
  b. an absolute symphony based on classical forms
  c. a symphonic poem based on a loose program

3. How many variations of the theme are heard in this movement?

   _____ Can you hear when each one begins? _____

4. Could this movement be viewed as repetitious? _____

   Explain your answer. _____

   _____

   _____

5. What provides the musical interest in this movement?

   _____

   _____

6. How would you describe the mood of this movement?

   _____

7. How many symphonies did Brahms write? _____

   Why did he wait until late in his life to write symphonies?

   _____

   _____

   _____

*Listen to the second movement of Dvořák's Symphony No. 9 (*From the New World*), and answer the following.

   8. How did this symphony get its subtitle, *From the New World?*

      _____

   9. What is "American" about the work? _____

      _____

  10. On what epic poem is it loosely based? _____

      _____ Have you read this poem? _____

  11. Is it necessary to know the poem to understand the form of the second

      movement? _____

  12. What instrument does Dvořák feature in the main theme of the

      movement? _____ Can you easily recognize the

      sound of this instrument? _____

  13. Is this symphony in standard sonata-cycle form? _____

      Are the keys of the movements standard? _____

  14. What works did Dvořák write that could be considered nationalistic?

      _____

      _____

  15. Describe what mood you perceive or picture you envisage when you

      listen to this movement of the *New World Symphony.*

      _____

      _____

      _____

62. *Exploring* Dvořák's Influence on African-American Art Music
(**CP** 13 C/Sh; 4 S)

Complete the following questions.

1. What types of traditional music interested Dvořák during his years in America? _____

_____

2. What famous American poem is loosely the basis for Dvořák's *New World Symphony?* _____

Who is the poet? _____

3. Which spiritual was Dvořák especially fond of?

_____

4. What challenge did Dvořák issue to American composers?

_____

_____

_____

5. For what is Dvořák's student Henry Burleigh known today?

_____

_____

_____

6. Which well-known African-American composer rose to Dvořák's challenge? _____

How did he accomplish this? _____

_____

_____

_____

7. Which white American composer is famous for his wedding of jazz to art music? _____

Which work demonstrates this? _____

Music listening assignment: Listen to a recording of one movement from William Grant Still's *Afro-American* Symphony and describe how it imitates blues, jazz, spirituals, or other traditional African-American music styles and instruments. (Alternate works include Still's Suite for Violin and Piano, third movement; Gershwin's *Rhapsody in Blue* or Concerto in F; or a spiritual arrangement).

Selection: _____

Composer: _____

What African-American music styles do you think influenced this work?

_____

_____

_____

What musical elements in particular have influenced the style?

_____

_____

_____

_____

_____

_____

Other comments about style: _____

_____

_____

_____

_____

_____

_____

_____

63. *Listening* Robert Schumann and the Romantic Concerto*
*Robert Schumann: Piano Concerto in A minor, Op. 54, First Movement
(**LG** 47 C; 12 S)

*Listen to the first movement of Robert Schumann's Piano Concerto in A minor, and answer the following.

1. What was the original title of this work? _____

   _____

   When did he write this? _____ When did he write the

   remaining movements? _____

2. What instrument introduces the main theme in the first movement?

   _____ In what key is it presented? _____

3. How does theme 2 differ from theme 1? _____

   _____

4. Who wrote the cadenza for this work? _____

5. What is the overall form of the first movement?

   _____

6. From where does the idea for the coda theme come?

   _____

7. Does the "double exposition" idea of the Classical concerto apply to this

   work? _____ Explain. _____

   _____

8. Do the remaining movements fit the standard concerto scheme?

   _____

9. Does the concerto begin and end in the same key? _____

   Explain. _____

   _____

10. What effect does the minor key have on the character of the first

    movement? _____

    _____

About the Composer

11. Why was Robert Schumann unable to be a concert pianist?

_____

12. Which woman pianist furthered his works in performance?

_____

13. What music journal did Schumann found? _____

14. What was Schumann's "year of song"? _____

    Why was it called that? _____

15. What kind of illness did Robert Schumann develop in later years?

_____

    What would be the likely diagnosis of his illness today?

_____

16. Name two song cycles by Robert Schumann and the poets on which
    they are based.

_____

_____

17. Name some titles of piano works by Schumann.

_____

18. What type of piano work did he prefer? _____

_____

19. In what large-scale forms did Schumann write?

_____

_____

65. *Reviewing* Opera in the Nineteenth Century
(Chap. 57 C; 53 Sh; 28 S)

Complete the following questions.

1. Describe the following parts of an opera, giving consideration to musical style and purpose within the plot.

    a. Aria: _____

    _____

    b. Recitative: _____

    _____

    c. Chorus: _____

    _____

    d. Ensemble: _____

    _____

2. What is the role of the orchestra in an opera? _____

    _____

3. What is a libretto, and who writes it? _____

    _____

Match the following styles of opera with their definitions on the right.

_____ 4. grand opera   a. light German opera featuring spoken dialogue

_____ 5. opéra comique   b. Italian version of comic opera

_____ 6. Singspiel   c. hybrid opera type with appealing melodies and romantic dramatic spectacle

_____ 7. opera seria   d. French opera style, featuring historical subjects and huge forces

_____ 8. opera buffa   e. Italian singing style, featuring florid lines and pure voices

_____ 9. bel canto   f. French comic opera, with simple plots and spoken dialogue

_____ 10. lyric opera   g. Italian serious opera

Match the following well-known operas with their composers (look up the principal works of these composers in the following chapters).

____ 11. *Die Meistersinger von Nürnberg*   a. Giuseppe Verdi

____ 12. *Aïda*   b. Richard Wagner

____ 13. *Otello*   c. Giacomo Puccini

____ 14. *Madame Butterfly*

____ 15. *Tristan and Isolde*

____ 16. *Turandot*

____ 17. *Rigoletto*

18. What makes an opera "exotic"? _____

_____

    Name an example. _____

19. Name an opera composed by a woman. _____

    Who was the composer? _____

    What was the basis of the plot? _____

20. Which famous soprano was known as the "Swedish nightingale"?

_____

    Who managed her career in America?_____

21. What was the relationship between Maria Malibran and Pauline Viardot?

_____

22. Which composers' works did they specialize in singing?

    Malibran: _____

    Viardot: _____

23. Did opera further the careers of women musicians in this era? _____

    Explain. _____

_____

_____

---

66. *Listening* **Verdi and Wagner**
Verdi: *La traviata*, Act II, Finale (**LG** 49 C; 26 Sh; 14 S)
Wagner: *Die Walküre* (**LG** 50 C; 27 Sh; 15 S)

Listen to the excerpt from *La traviata*, and answer the following.

1. What literary work provided the basis for *La traviata?*

_____

2. What makes Violetta a typical Romantic heroine?_____

_____

3. How does the opera reach a musical climax at the end of Act II?

_____

_____

4. Describe the emotions each character is expressing in this excerpt.

Violetta: _____   Alfredo: _____

Germont: _____   Baron: _____

Chorus: _____

5. How would you describe Verdi's melodic style (in his arias)?

_____

6. Why do you think Verdi's operas have remained so popular?

_____

About the Composer

7. In what country was Verdi born? _____

8. Which Verdi operas were inspired by Shakespeare?

_____

9. Which of his operas could be described as "exotic"?

_____

10. What was his last great opera?_____

Listen to the excerpt from *Die Walküre* and answer the following.

11. What is the basis for the story of this opera? _____

12. Who is Wotan? _____

    Brunnhilde? _____

13. Describe the following musical themes in your own words.

    *Wotan's farewell: _____

    Wotan's invocation of Loge: _____

    "Magic fire" music: _____

    "Magic sleep" music: _____

Tru or False

____ 14. Wagner's operas reflect his desire to link music and drama closely.

____ 15. His operas have the same individual components—arias, recitatives, and ensembles—as Verdi's.

____ 16. *The Ring of the Nibelung* is a cycle of four operas.

____ 17. Wagner strove to achieve an endless melody that was melded to the German language.

____ 18. The orchestra was unimportant to Wagner's music dramas.

____ 19. Wagner employed recurring themes called Leitmotifs.

____ 20. Wagner's harmonic style was a conservative, diatonic one.

21. What are some of Wagner's operas written prior to *The Ring*?

    _____

    _____

22. What festival was established for the performance of Wagner's operas?

    _____

23. With whom did Wagner find happiness late in his life?

    _____

---

67. *Exploring* The Lure of Spain
(**CP** 14 C/Sh; 5 S)

Complete the following questions.

1. What culture is featured in Bizet's opera *Carmen?* _____

   In which country is the opera set? _____

2. What elements of *Carmen* did nineteenth-century audiences find

   shocking? _____

3. What could be viewed as "exotic" about Bizet's *Carmen?*

   _____

   _____

   _____

4. Explain the focus of the nineteenth-century movement known as

   naturalism._____

   _____

   Which French writer was a leader in this movement? _____

5. What are the musical characteristics of flamenco music?

   _____

   _____

   _____

   What instruments are used in flamenco performance?_____

   _____

   What musical culture influenced flamenco singing style?

   _____

6. What is a habanera? _____

   What is its origin? _____

7. Which twentieth-century Latin American dance form did the habanera

   influence? _____ What is the character of this dance?

   _____

Essay: Select either A or B below.

    A. Locate a recorded example (or video) of flamenco music, listen to a selection, and describe as many elements of its style as you can (especially its rhythm, melody, and instruments). If you have a video, describe the dance movements as well as the music.

    B. Watch a video of the 1992 movie *Scent of a Woman* (available in many libraries or at the video store), focusing on the scene where actor Al Pacino dances a tango. Describe in detail the music for this dance scene (especially the rhythms and tempo) and the movements of the tango as portrayed in the movie.

_____

_____

_____

_____

_____

_____

_____

_____

_____

_____

_____

_____

_____

_____

_____

_____

_____

_____

_____

_____

_____

68. *Listening* Late Romantic Opera and Exoticism
*Bizet: *Carmen*, Act I, excerpt (**LG** 51 C; 16 S)
Leoncavallo: *Pagliacci*, Act I, Canio's Aria (**LG** 52 C; 28 Sh; 17 S)

*Listen to the excerpt from Bizet's *Carmen*, and answer the following.

1. What is the literary basis for *Carmen*? _____
_____

2. How does Bizet evoke the feeling of a march in Act I?
_____

3. What role does the chorus play in Act I?
_____
_____

4. What kind of rhythmic accompaniment is heard in Carmen's aria?
_____

5. What is seductive about this character and her music?
_____
_____

6. Is Carmen a likable character? _____ Explain.
_____
_____

7. What is the structure of Carmen's habanera?
_____
_____

8. What gives this opera its dramatic impact? _____
_____

9. In your opinion, what accounts for the popularity of this opera?
_____
_____

Listen to Canio's aria from *Pagliacci,* and answer the following.

10. Who wrote the libretto for *Pagliacci?* _____

    What is its basis? _____

11. What earlier dramatic tradition does this opera and its characters

    evoke? _____

12. Describe the character of Pagliaccio in your own words.

    _____

13. What distinguishes the musical style of the aria ("Vesti la giubba") from

    the recitative ("Recitar")? _____

    _____

14. What gives this aria its highly dramatic mood? _____

    _____

15. Name the "Three Tenors," all of whom have sung this aria.

    _____

    _____

16. What was the public's reaction to this opera? _____

    _____

17. What other composers carried on the late-Romantic Italian operatic

    tradition? _____

18. What was the movement known as verismo? _____

    _____

19. Which literary figures were associated with this movement?

    _____

> **69. *Reviewing* Tchaikovsky and the Ballet**
> (Chap. 62 C; 57 Sh; 33 S)

True or False

____ 1. Renaissance entertainments included elaborate dance sequences as part of theatrical productions.

____ 2. Classical ballet was first developed in the Romantic era by the Russians.

____ 3. Stravinsky and Diaghilev were famous Russian dancers.

____ 4. The *pas de deux*, or dance for two, developed in Russia by the choreographer Petipa, is a standard element of classical ballet.

____ 5. Tchaikovsky and Petipa worked together on *The Nutcracker*.

Complete the following questions.

6. What three well-known ballets did Tchaikovsky write?

   a. _____

   b. _____

   c. _____

7. *The Nutcracker* was based on a story originally written by the Romantic

   writer _____ and expanded by

   _____.

About the Composer

8. What teaching position did Tchaikovsky hold in Russia?

   _____

9. How did Tchaikovsky feel about his homosexuality?

   _____

10. What role did Nadezhda von Meck play in the composer's life?

   _____

11. What was the reaction of Western audiences to Tchaikovsky's music?

   _____

   _____

12. In addition to his ballets, in which other musical forms did Tchaikovsky write? _____

_____

The Nutcracker

13. What is the setting for *The Nutcracker*? _____

_____

14. Who are the main characters? _____

_____

15. How do the "exotic" Arab and Chinese dances fit into the story of the ballet? _____

_____

16. How does Tchaikovsky set a different mood for each dance?

_____

*17. Describe the character of each of the following dances.

March: _____

Dance of the Sugar Plum Fairy: _____

_____

Trepak: _____

18. Have you ever seen a performance of *The Nutcracker*? _____

If yes, was it ___ live, ___ on TV, or ___ on video?

Did you enjoy it? _____ What do you think accounts for the continued popularity of this classical ballet?

_____

_____

138

70. *Reviewing* The Post-Romantic Era and Impressionism
(Trans. V C/Sh/S; Chap. 63 C/S; 58 Sh)

Complete the following questions.

1. What are the approximate dates of the post-Romantic era? _____

2. Which Italian operatic composers can be associated with post-Romanticism? _____

3. Which Germanic composers can be associated with post-Romanticism?

_____

4. What are some post-Romantic characteristics heard in the music of these composers? _____

_____

5. What are some of the national schools that rose to prominence in this era? _____

Multiple Choice

____ 6. Which is <u>not</u> <u>true</u> of the origins of Impressionism?
   a. It was first a term denoting scorn of the new style.
   b. The coining of the term was based on a painting by Claude Monet.
   c. The style was first popular in Italy.
   d. A school of artists developed, all wishing to capture first impressions on canvas.

____ 7. Who among these is <u>not</u> an Impressionist painter?
   a. Paul Klee
   b. Camille Pissarro
   c. Edgar Degas
   d. Auguste Renoir

____ 8. The parallel movement in poetry toward suggestion rather than direct description was called:
   a. Expressionism.
   b. New Romanticism.
   c. Symbolism.
   d. minimalism.

____ 9. Who was the American poet who strongly influenced the literary movement referred to in question #8 above?
   a. Charles Baudelaire
   b. Edgar Allan Poe
   c. Stéphane Mallarmé
   d. Paul Verlaine

10. What were some goals of Impressionist painters?

_____

_____

_____

11. Describe the characteristics of Impressionist painting in your own
    words. Base your description on the Monet painting *Impression: Sun
    Rising*, reproduced in the text.

_____

_____

_____

12. Characterize the elements of Impressionist music below.

    Melody/scales: _____

    _____

    Rhythm/meter: _____

    _____

    Harmony/dissonance: _____

    _____

    Form: _____

    _____

13. In what ways did non-Western music influence Impressionism?

_____

_____

14. In what ways did Impressionism look back to early musical styles?

_____

_____

15. Which composer best exemplifies musical Impressionism?

_____

71. *Listening* Mahler and Strauss*
*Mahler: *The Song of the Earth,* Third Movement (**LG** 54 C/S)
*Strauss: *Der Rosenkavalier,* Act III, Trio (**LG** 55 C/S)

*Listen to the third movement from Mahler's *Song of the Earth,* and answer the following questions.

1. What is the literary basis for *The Song of the Earth*?

   _____

2. What is the medium (performing forces) for this song cycle?

   _____

3. How does Mahler evoke the sounds of Chinese music in this work?

   _____

   _____

4. How does the text evoke images of China? _____

   _____

5. Does this work sound "exotic" to you? _____

   Explain. _____

About the Composer

6. What important musical positions did Mahler hold? _____

   _____

7. Why did Mahler convert from Judaism to Catholicism?

   _____

8. How many symphonies did Mahler write? _____

9. What other song cycles did he write? _____

   _____

10. What elements of Mahler's style could be viewed as Romantic?

    _____

    _____

*Listen to the Trio from *Der Rosenkavalier* by Richard Strauss, and answer the following questions.

11. What is the setting (place, era) for *Der Rosenkavalier?*

_____

12. How does the story reflect the title (Cavalier of the Rose)?

_____

_____

13. Describe each of the following characters in the opera, and suggest what emotion each is expressing in the Trio.

Octavian: _____

_____

Marschallin: _____

_____

Sophie: _____

_____

14. Which male character is sung by a woman in the opera?

_____ Why? _____

_____

15. What is virtuosic or demanding about the singing style for these roles?

_____

About the Composer

16. What musical role did Strauss play during the Nazi regime, and why was it controversial? _____

_____

_____

17. Name several of his well-known symphonic poems: _____

_____

18. Name several other operas by Strauss: _____

_____

> **72. *Exploring* Vienna at the Turn of the Century**
> (**CP** 15 C/Sh/S)

Complete the following questions

1. What Eastern cultures were influential to the arts in turn-of-the-century Vienna? _____

2. What contribution did architect Adolf Loos make to artistic trends?

   _____

   _____

3. Name a famous example of Bauhaus style: _____
   Who designed it? _____

4. What elements of Chinese poetry were especially interesting to the Viennese? _____

   _____

   Which Chinese poet was especially influential? _____

5. In which composition did Mahler emulate Chinese music?

   _____

   How did he make his music sound Chinese? _____

   _____

   _____

6. Who was the leader of the second Viennese school of composition?

   _____

7. What are some of Vienna's great musical institutions?

   _____

   _____

   _____

   With which one was Mahler associated? _____

8. For which styles of music is Vienna known today? _____

   _____

Music listening assignment: Locate a recording of Chinese or Japanese music (check in your library, or ask your instructor for one from the Music Example Bank). Listen to it, and describe the following elements below.

Describe the character of the melodic line. _____

_____

_____

What kind of scale is the melody based on? _____

_____

Describe the character of the rhythm and meter. _____

_____

_____

Describe the harmony (if any). _____

_____

_____

Describe the texture. _____

_____

_____

Describe the instruments heard. _____

_____

_____

_____

Describe the vocal style (if sung). _____

_____

_____

Comments: _____

_____

_____

---

73. *Listening* **Debussy and Ravel**
 Debussy: *Prelude to "The Afternoon of a Faun"* (**LG** 56 C/S; 29 Sh)
 *Ravel: *Songs of Madagascar*, Second Movement (**LG** 57 C/S)

Listen to Debussy's *Prelude to "The Afternoon of a Faun,"* and answer the following questions.

1. What is the literary source for this Debussy work?

   _____

2. Summarize briefly the program for this work. _____

   _____

   _____

3. In your opinion, how does Debussy musically evoke images from the

   poem? _____

   _____

   _____

4. What Impressionistic traits do you hear in this work?

   Melody/rhythm: _____

   Harmony/texture: _____

   Form: _____

   Timbre/color: _____

   Other: _____

5. How does Debussy vary slightly the return of the opening material?

   _____

   _____

6. What types of orchestral forms did Debussy favor? _____

   _____

7. What opera did Debussy write that is based on a Symbolist drama?

   _____

*Listen to "Do Not Trust the White Men" from Ravel's *Songs of Madagascar*, and answer the following.

8. What is the source for the texts for this song cycle?

   _____

9. Who commissioned this work? _____

10. What is the medium? _____

11. How authentic is the poetic and musical description of this African

    nation? _____

    How authentic is the general sentiment expressed by the text?

    _____

12. How does Ravel musically evoke the powerful drama of this text?

    _____

    _____

13. Describe the vocal style used in this song. _____

    _____

14. Where does the song reach its musical climax? _____

    _____

15. What was the public's reaction to this song cycle, and why?

    _____

    _____

16. How does Ravel's musical style differ from that of Debussy?

    _____

    _____

    _____

> **74.** *Exploring* **The Paris World Exhibition of 1889: A Cultural Awakening** (**CP** 16 C/Sh/S)

Complete the following questions.

1. What was the famous monument built for the Paris World Exhibition of 1889? _____

2. What is a gamelan orchestra? _____

_____

_____

Where was the gamelan from that Debussy heard? _____

3. What elements of gamelan music did Debussy try to imitate in his composition? _____

_____

_____

4. Which other countries were represented by musicians at this world exhibition? _____

_____

_____

5. What Middle Eastern styles of dancing were seen at this event?

_____

6. What is a cakewalk? _____

_____

Where did it originate? _____

7. What other traditional music styles were influential to Debussy?

_____

_____

8. What flamenco techniques did Debussy imitate in his piano works?

_____

_____

Music listening assignment: Locate a recording (or video) of a gamelan (from Java or Bali) in your library (or ask your instructor for one from the Music Example Bank). Listen to a selection and describe the music below. Be sure to read any notes available about the work.

Which country is the gamelan from? _____

What are the instruments heard? Describe how they sound.

_____

_____

_____

_____

_____

_____

_____

Describe the melodic line and rhythmic movement. _____

_____

_____

_____

Describe the texture and harmony heard. _____

_____

_____

_____

If you used a video, describe any dancing you saw. _____

_____

_____

Comments: _____

_____

_____

75. *Exploring* A Composer's World of Musical Styles
(**CP** 17 C/Sh/S)

Complete the following questions

1. What are some of the diverse musical cultures to which composer

    Maurice Ravel was attracted? _____

    _____

    _____

2. In which region of France was Ravel born? _____

3. What types of Spanish music and dance interested Ravel?

    _____

    _____

4. What is Spanish about Ravel's famous work *Boléro?* _____

    _____

    What is its musical basis? _____

    _____

5. What cultural event was influential to Ravel's musical tastes?

    _____

6. From which culture does Ravel's *Shéhérazade* draw inspiration?

    _____

7. How does Ravel evoke Far Eastern culture in his *Mother Goose* Suite?

    _____

    _____

    _____

8. What American popular styles did Ravel imitate in his music?

    _____

9. How else did Ravel show his global musical interests?

    _____

    _____

Music listening assignment: Select one of the following works by Maurice Ravel, listen to a recording of it, and describe the musical elements that make it sound "exotic" or reminiscent of a particular music culture.

> *Boléro* (Spain)
> *Rapsodie espagnole* (Spain)
> *Tzigane* (Gypsy or Romany)
> Violin Sonata, Second Movement (blues)
> *Shéhérazade* (Asian)

Work chosen: _____

Description: _____

Melodic characteristics: _____

_____

_____

Rhythmic characteristics: _____

_____

_____

_____

Texture and timbre: _____

_____

_____

_____

_____

Other style traits: _____

_____

_____

_____

_____

_____

76. *Reviewing* Elements of Twentieth-Century Musical Style
(Chap. 65–66 C/S; 59–60 Sh)

Multiple Choice

____ 1. In which element of music was primitivism most evident?
a. melody
b. rhythm
c. texture
d. harmony

____ 2. Which is not true of Expressionism?
a. It was principally a French movement.
b. It attempted to probe the subconscious.
c. It defied traditional notions of beauty.
d. It portrayed images in distortion.

____ 3. Which is most typical of Expressionist music?
a. conjunct, symmetrical melodies
b. instruments used in extreme high and low registers
c. consonant, tonal harmonies
d. regular meters and rhythms

____ 4. Which is most typical of the New Classicism?
a. an emotional, expressive style
b. a focus on program music
c. a preference for absolute music
d. an attempt to bring music and poetry closer

Match the following early twentieth-century figures with the correct
description on the right.

____ 5. Paul Gauguin   a. Expressionist composer

____ 6. Marcel Duchamp   b. Expressionist writer

____ 7. Franz Kafka   c. Expressionist painter

____ 8. Wassily Kandinsky   d. French painter drawn to primitive
                                     subjects

____ 9. Arnold Schoenberg   e. Surrealist painter

____ 10. Salvador Dali   f. Cubist painter

____ 11. Pablo Picasso   g. Dadaist artist

12. Which early twentieth-century movement influenced electronic music

composer Edgard Varèse? _____

13. What early twentieth-century figures were influential to avant-garde composer John Cage? _____

Match the following musical terms with their definitions on the right.

____ 14. polyrhythm   a. a particular arrangement of the twelve chromatic tones

____ 15. dissonant counterpoint   b. the use of two or more keys together

____ 16. polytonality   c. the tendency to elevate form above expression

____ 17. serial music   d. the simultaneous use of several rhythmic patterns

____ 18. tone row   e. the use of dissonant intervals to set musical lines apart

____ 19. formalism   f. the rejection of any key or tonality

____ 20. atonality   g. music based on the twelve-tone method

True or False

____ 21. The term "dodecaphonic" refers to the use of tonality.

____ 22. In twentieth-century music, dissonances do not always resolve.

____ 23. Orchestras grew even larger in the early twentieth century.

____ 24. Twentieth-century melodies are generally more difficult to sing than those of the Romantic era.

____ 25. The use of triads continued to predominate early twentieth-century music.

____ 26. Schoenberg is generally credited with founding the twelve-tone method of composition.

____ 27. Tone rows were often transposed so they began on other notes.

____ 28. Early twentieth-century music remained consonant to the ear.

____ 29. Duple, triple, and quadruple meter were the norm in the early twentieth century.

____ 30. Inversion refers to the mirror-image movement of a line, wherein each interval moves in the opposite direction of the original.

____ 31. The contrapuntal devices used in tone row manipulation were the same as those used in the Baroque fugue.

____ 32. Dark or low instruments were explored by early twentieth-century composers.

---

77. *Listening* Stravinsky's *Petrushka*
(**LG** 58 C/S; 30 Sh)

Listen to the first tableau of *Petrushka,* and answer the questions below.

1. What is the setting for the ballet *Petrushka?* _____

_____

2. Who is the character Petrushka? _____

What is he called in other languages? _____

Who are the other characters? _____

3. How does Stravinsky evoke the crowd scene at the opening?

_____

How does this musical idea unify the first part of this work?

_____

4. Which melodies are most memorable in the first tableau?

_____

What is folklike about them? _____

_____

5. Describe how the term "percussive harmony" applies to this excerpt.

_____

_____

6. How would you characterize the rhythmic treatment in this work?

_____

_____

What difficulties did the original dancers have with the rhythm and meter?

_____

7. What is nationalistic about *Petrushka?* _____

_____

About the Composer

8. Where was Stravinsky born? _____

Where was *Petrushka* premiered? _____

9. Who commissioned *Petrushka?* _____

Name two other ballets commissioned by the same individual.

a. _____ b. _____

10. Which famous dancers performed the premiere of *Petrushka?*

_____

11. Where did Stravinsky live after World War I? _____

after World War II? _____

12. Consider Stravinsky's total output, then name an example for each of the following (excluding *Petrushka*):

a. A Russian nationalistic work: _____

b. A Neoclassical work: _____

c. A twelve-tone work: _____

d. A major choral work: _____

e. An opera: _____

13. What do you believe accounts for the greatness of Stravinsky's music?

_____

_____

_____

_____

_____

---

78. *Exploring Petrushka* and Russian Folk Traditions
(**CP** 18 C/Sh/S)

Complete the following questions.

1. Which nineteenth-century Russian composer compiled collections of his native folk songs? _____

2. Name two ballets by Stravinsky that make use of Russian folk material.

    a. _____   b. _____

3. What is the historical significance of Carnival celebrations?

    _____

    _____

    _____

    Where do famous Carnival celebrations take place today?

    _____

4. What Easter morning tradition followed in Russia is described in the *Song of the Volochebniki?* _____

    _____

    _____

    _____

    Describe the character of this song. _____

    _____

5. What event is celebrated on Midsummer Night? _____

    _____

6. What traditions have arisen to celebrate Midsummer Night?

    _____

    _____

    _____

7. Which famous play takes place on this evening?

    _____

Music listening assignment: Select A or B below.

A. Listen to a recording of a Russian folk song (check your library or ask your instructor for one from the Music Example Bank). Describe the song text and musical style below. Try to determine what elements are typically Russian.

B. Listen to a recording of one of the Russian orchestral compositions below, which borrow from Russian folk song or folklore. Read about the legend or basis for the work, and describe how the music depicts the story and its Russian setting.

> Rimsky-Korsakov, *Russian Easter* Overture (based on Russian devotional songs)
> Rimsky-Korsakov, *The Golden Cockerel*
> Rimsky-Korsakov, *Skazka (Baba-Yaga,* the witch in Russian folklore)
> Stravinsky, *The Firebird* (a magical tale about good, evil, and supernatural beings)

Selection: _____

Composer/Performers: _____

Description of work: _____

_____

_____

_____

_____

_____

_____

_____

_____

_____

_____

_____

_____

_____

_____

_____

_____

_____

80. *Reviewing* Nationalism in the Twentieth Century
(Chap. 71–72 C/S; 63–64 Sh)

Match the following composers with their nationalistic school on the right.
(You may use answers as many times as necessary.)

_____ 1. Benjamin Britten   a. French school

_____ 2. Paul Hindemith   b. German school

_____ 3. Charles Ives   c. Russian school

_____ 4. Sergei Rachmaninoff   d. English school

_____ 5. Béla Bartók   e. Hungarian school

_____ 6. Carl Orff   f. Scandinavian school

_____ 7. Dmitri Shostakovich   g. American school

_____ 8. Francis Poulenc   h. Spanish school

_____ 9. Jean Sibelius

_____ 10. Sergei Prokofiev

_____ 11. Manuel de Falla

_____ 12. Ralph Vaughan Williams

_____ 13. Ruth Crawford

14. For each of the countries below, suggest a historical event or
    nationalistic theme or setting that either served or could have served as
    the basis for a musical composition:

    a. Russia: _____

    b. France: _____

    c. Germany: _____

    d. England: _____

    e. United States: _____

15. What were the goals of the French group known as *Les Six?*

    _____

    Who was the only female member of this group?_____

16. Name a composer and work linked to Jewish cultural origins.

    _____

True or False

____ 17. American concert life in the nineteenth century was dominated by European musicians.

____ 18. The spiritual is of European origin.

____ 19. The music of some European nationalist composers features folk elements.

____ 20. The piano music of Louis Gottschalk features Native American elements.

____ 21. The American composer Charles Ives was from California.

22. Describe why nineteenth-century America could be considered a "melting pot" of musical styles.

_____

_____

_____

23. What musical style(s) contributed to the beginnings of American nationalism?

_____

_____

_____

24. Describe briefly the style of each of these early American composers.

   a. William Billings: _____

   b. Stephen Foster: _____

   c. Louis Gottschalk: _____

   d. Charles Griffes: _____

> ## 81. *Listening* Prokofiev and Bartók
> *Prokofiev: *Alexander Nevsky,* Seventh Movement (**LG** 62 C/S)
> Bartók: *Music for Strings, Percussion, and Celesta,* Fourth Movement
> (**LG** 63 C/S; 32 Sh)

*Listen to the excerpt from *Alexander Nevsky,* and respond below.

1. What is the basis for Prokofiev's *Alexander Nevsky?*

   _____

2. Who directed the film for which this music was originally written?

   _____ When was it made?_____

   When was this music reworked into a cantata? _____

3. How did the film *Alexander Nevsky* and its music serve to bolster the

   morale of the Russians? _____

   _____

4. What aspects of the last movement of the cantata *Alexander Nevsky*

   sound particularly Russian? _____

   _____

   _____

   Can you follow the Russian text in the Listening Guide? _____

About the Composer

5. What political pressures did Prokofiev run up against in his career?

   _____

   _____

6. What elements of Classicism are heard in Prokofiev's music?

   _____

7. Through which elements did he strive for innovation?

   _____

8. Name several well-known works by Prokofiev. _____

   _____

Listen to the last movement of Bartók's *Music for Strings, Percussion, and Celesta*, and respond below.

9. What is the medium for this work? _____

_____

What is unusual about this ensemble's makeup? _____

_____

10. Describe the character of the opening of the movement.

Melody: _____

Rhythm: _____

Harmony: _____

11. What type of folk dance style does this movement imitate?

_____

12. What is the form of this movement? _____

13. What types of contrapuntal techniques does Bartók employ in this

movement? _____

_____

14. Consider the composer's output as a whole, and check those elements (one per pair) that best define his style.

___ a. use of free forms or

___ b. use of traditional forms

___ c. rhythmic complexity or

___ d. rhythmic simplicity

___ e. modal harmonies or

___ f. major and minor harmonies

___ g. traditional orchestration or

___ h. innovative orchestration

82. *Exploring* Bartók—a Roving Collector of Folk Songs
(**CP** 19 C/Sh/S)

Complete the following questions.

1. What were the goals of composers Béla Bartók and Zoltán Kodály in collecting Eastern European folk songs? _____

   _____

   _____

2. What is an ethnomusicologist? _____

   _____

3. What does it mean to do "fieldwork"? _____

   _____

4. How was Bartók's art music influenced by the traditional music he collected? _____

   _____

   _____

5. What is an additive meter? _____

   _____

   _____

6. What is the background of the Romany people and their musical traditions? _____

   _____

   _____

   _____

   What are they popularly called? _____

7. What nineteenth-century Hungarian composer was interested in Romany music? _____ What evidence do we have of this interest? _____

   _____

Music listening assignment: Listen to a recording of modern Romany (Gypsy) music (find one in your library or ask your instructor for one from the Music Example Bank). Answer the following questions.

Name of ensemble (if known): _____

What instruments are heard? _____

_____

_____

Describe the melodic and rhythmic style. _____

_____

_____

_____

Describe the tempo. _____

_____

Describe the harmony. _____

_____

_____

Describe the singing (if any). _____

_____

_____

Other comments: _____

_____

_____

_____

_____

_____

_____

---

83. *Listening* **Ives, Crawford, and Copland**
  *Ives: *The Fourth of July,* from *A Symphony: New England Holidays* (**LG** 64 C/S)
  *Crawford: *Rat Riddles,* from Three Songs (**LG** 65 C/S)
  Copland: *Street in a Frontier Town,* from *Billy the Kid* (**LG** 66 C/S; 33 Sh)

---

*Listen to *The Fourth of July* by Ives, and respond below.

  1. What images does Ives attempt to evoke in this work?

  _____

  _____

  2. What musical elements can be viewed as nationalistic?

  _____

  _____

  3. What tunes can you actually recognize in the work?

  _____

  4. How would you characterize his treatment of harmony?

  _____

  5. Charles Ives is viewed today as one of the great twentieth-century
     American composers. How was his music received by the public during
     his lifetime?

  _____

  _____

*Listen to *Rat Riddles* by Ruth Crawford, and respond below.

  6. This song sets a poem by the American poet: _____

  7. What is the poem about? _____

  8. How does the music depict the comic, whimsical nature of the poem?

  _____

  9. Describe the vocal style. _____

  10. What Baroque formal procedure does Crawford use in this song?

  _____

  11. To what kind of musical studies did Ruth Crawford devote her later life?

  _____

Listen to the *Street in a Frontier Town* scene from Copland's *Billy the Kid*, and respond below.

12. Briefly describe the story of Billy the Kid. _____

_____

_____

13. Suggest how each musical element below supports the story.

   Melody: _____

   Rhythm/meter: _____

   Harmony: _____

   Choice of instruments: _____

   _____

14. How does the composer evoke a Mexican dance scene?

   _____

   _____

15. Do you recognize any of the tunes Copland uses in this work? _____

   If yes, which? _____

16. Does he use the tunes literally? _____ Explain.

   _____

17. List two other ballets by Copland, and tell how each is nationalistic.

   a. _____

   _____

   b. _____

   _____

18. How did Copland gain his familiarity with American folk music?

   _____

   _____

   _____

---

84. *Exploring* Music and the Patriotic Spirit
(**CP** 20 C/Sh/S)

Complete the following questions.

1. What famous tunes were sung during the Revolutionary and Civil Wars?

   _____

   _____

2. What Civil War song text was written by Julia Ward Howe?

   _____

3. Which twentieth-century songwriter provided the music and words to

   Over There? _____ During which war was this

   popular? _____

4. Which well-known patriotic song, made famous by singer Kate Smith, is

   viewed as a second national anthem in the United States?

   _____

5. Describe when and by whom the lyrics for *The Star-Spangled Banner* were

   written. _____

   _____

   _____

   _____

6. Which national anthems can be viewed as songs of war or independence?

   _____

   _____

7. What is the origin of the tune to Austria's *Emperor's Hymn?*

   _____

   Which other country has adopted this song? _____

8. What is the Canadian national anthem? _____

   Who wrote it and when? _____

Activity: Watch a video (from the library or video store) of the 1942 film classic *Yankee Doodle Dandy*, starring James Cagney (as George M. Cohan). Focus on several of the songs from the show, and answer the questions below.

Which songs are especially patriotic? _____

_____

_____

How are their texts inspirational? _____

_____

_____

Explain how the music could be viewed as nationalistic.

_____

_____

_____

_____

_____

When did George M. Cohan live? _____

During which historical event was this movie set? _____

During which historical event was this movie made? _____

Comments on the film: _____

_____

_____

_____

_____

_____

85. *Exploring* Copland Looks to the Wild West and South of the Border (CP 21 C/Sh/S)

Complete the following questions.

1. What American themes did composer Aaron Copland incorporate in his music? _____

   _____

2. What aspects of cowboy life do their songs tell of? _____

   _____

   _____

3. Name several historical American cowboys and cowgirls.

   _____

   _____

4. Which woman was the subject of the Broadway musical *Annie Get Your Gun?* _____

5. Who was the "yellow rose of Texas," and why was she so famous?

   _____

   _____

   _____

   _____

6. Which American artist is well-known for his cowboy bronzes?

   _____

7. Describe the Mexican jarabe. _____

   _____

   _____

8. Describe a mariachi ensemble. _____

   _____

   _____

Music listening assignment: Select either A or B below. (Recordings for both assignments are in the Music Example Bank.)

A. Locate a recording of historical or contemporary cowboy songs. Historical songs might be sung by Roy Rogers, Tex Ritter, or Gene Autry; contemporary recordings are available by Michael Martin Murphey, Chris Ledoux (he writes his own), and Johnny Cash. Listen to several selections, and describe below the subjects of the songs, the melodies and singing style, and the accompaniment used.

B. Locate a recording of a Mexican mariachi ensemble. Listen to several selections, and describe below the instruments heard, the melodic and rhythmic style, and any vocals heard.

_____

_____

_____

_____

_____

_____

_____

_____

_____

_____

_____

_____

_____

_____

_____

_____

_____

_____

_____

_____

86. *Reviewing* **Blues and Jazz**
(Chap. 73–74 C/S; 65–66 Sh)

Complete the following questions.

1. What styles merged to form early jazz? _____

_____

2. What is ragtime? _____

_____

   Who is considered the "king of ragtime"? _____

   What famous rags did he write? _____

3. What is the typical poetic form of a blues text?

_____

_____

4. Write one verse of your own that could be sung to the blues.

_____

_____

_____

5. What is the standard musical form in blues? _____

_____

6. What is a "blue note"? _____

7. Name two great female blues singers. _____

_____

8. Which instruments would generally be heard in New Orleans jazz?

_____

_____

9. How does big band jazz differ from New Orleans jazz? _____

_____

10. What are some later styles of jazz, from the 1950s on?

_____

True or False

____ 11. New Orleans-style jazz spread across the country in the 1920s.

____ 12. Louis Armstrong was a noted jazz trombone player.

____ 13. West Coast jazz developed in the 1930s.

____ 14. A riff is a short melodic ostinato, or repeated passage, heard in jazz.

____ 15. Miles Davis can be associated with cool- and fusion-style jazz.

____ 16. Gerry Mulligan is a great baritone saxophone player.

____ 17. Dizzy Gillespie and Thelonious Monk developed the style known as bebop.

____ 18. The Gerry Mulligan Quartet is associated with big band jazz.

____ 19. Grateful Dead guitarist Jerry Garcia is also a noted jazz performer.

Match the following jazz styles with the best description on the right.

____ 20. New Orleans jazz

____ 21. big band jazz

____ 22. bebop

____ 23. cool jazz

____ 24. West Coast jazz

____ 25. third stream

____ 26. fusion

a. restrained style with rich harmonies and moderate tempos and volume

b. style that combines classical and jazz

c. style with two-note phrase

d. style that combines jazz improvisation with rock amplification

e. large-ensemble style with sections of brass, reeds, and rhythm instruments

f. style related to cool jazz, with mixed timbres and contrapuntal improvisations

g. early jazz style featuring multiple improvisations with small ensemble

87. *Exploring* The Roots of Jazz
(**CP** 22 C/Sh/S)

Complete the following questions.

1. From which cultures does jazz draw musical elements?

   _____

   _____

2. What singing styles still heard in certain African-American communities
   have African origins? _____

   _____

3. What is a work song? _____

   _____

4. What is a spiritual? _____

   _____

5. In which American city was jazz "born"? _____

6. What characterized nineteenth-century African-American music?

   _____

   _____

   _____

7. How did rural or country blues develop? _____

   _____

   _____

8. Describe ragtime and its rise to popularity. _____

   _____

   _____

   _____

9. Which art music composers were highly influenced by ragtime?

   _____

   _____

Music listening assignment: Listen to a recording of a spiritual (white or African-American), a vocal blues (Bessie Smith or Billie Holiday), or a rag (by Scott Joplin), and answer the questions below.

Work chosen: _____ Style: _____

Performers/Composer. _____

_____

Describe the melody and harmonic accompaniment. _____

_____

_____

Describe the rhythm and meter. _____

_____

_____

Describe the form. _____

_____

_____

Describe the text (if any). _____

_____

_____

What instruments are used? _____

_____

_____

Comments: _____

_____

_____

_____

_____

_____

_____

_____

88. *Listening* Louis Armstrong and Duke Ellington
West End Blues by Louis Armstrong and the Savoy Ballroom Five (**LG** 67 C/S)
Ellington: *Ko-Ko* (**LG** 68 C/S; 34 Sh)

*Listen to the recording of *West End Blues* by Louis Armstrong and the Savoy
Ballroom Five, and answer the following questions.

1. What style jazz does this represent? _____

2. Describe briefly the role of each of the instruments (consider solo vs.
   accompaniment and where the instrument is featured).

   Trumpet: _____

   Trombone: _____

   Clarinet: _____

   Banjo: _____

   Piano: _____

   Drums: _____

3. What is the form of the work? _____

   How many choruses are heard? _____ What repeats during each

   chorus? _____

   Can you follow the structure while listening? _____

4. What is scat singing? _____

   _____

   Where is it heard in this work? _____

   Who invented the style? _____

5. What other innovations are heard in this work? _____

   _____

6. Do you hear any "blue" notes in this work? _____

7. What was Louis Armstrong's nickname? _____

8. With which group did he play in 1925? _____

   Who was the pianist for this group? _____

Listen to *Ko-Ko* by Duke Ellington, and answer the following.

9. What style jazz does this represent? _____

10. What is the form of this work? _____

    How many choruses are heard? _____

11. What effect does the minor key create in this piece? _____

    _____

12. How is this ensemble different from a New Orleans group?

    _____

    What are the instrument families heard? _____

    _____

13. What percussion instrument dominates the work? _____

    What effect does this have? _____

    _____

14. Describe how the timbre of instruments is changed by mutes in this

    performance. _____

    _____

    _____

15. What instrument does Ellington play? _____

    Describe his performance style in this work. _____

    _____

    _____

16. What does it mean to say that this is "composed jazz"? _____

    _____

17. What elements make this work sound complex? _____

    _____

---

89. *Reviewing* American Musical Theater
(Chap. 74 C/S; 66 Sh)

Fill in the information below.

1. From which European stage genre did musical theater develop?

_____

2. Name a popular musical from the 1920s: _____

    from the 1930s: _____

    from the 1940s: _____

    from the 1950s: _____

3. List three musicals with a literary basis, and name the source for each:

    Musical   Basis

_____

_____

_____

4. Name two famous Broadway musical composer/songwriter teams and a show by each:

    Composer/Lyricist   Show

_____

_____

Match the following well-known musicals with their writers. (You may use a composer more than once.)

____ 5. *Into the Woods*   a. Stephen Sondheim

____ 6. *Les Misérables*   b. Andrew Lloyd Webber

____ 7. *Evita*   c. Claude-Michel Schonberg

____ 8. *Jesus Christ Superstar*

____ 9. *Cats*

____ 10. *Phantom of the Opera*

____ 11. *Sunset Boulevard*

____ 12. *Miss Saigon*

____ 13. *Sweeney Todd*

14. Name several classical musicals that have recently been revived on Broadway.

_____

_____

15. Name a musical that has a tragic ending: _____

16. Name a classic musical that deals with African-American life and uses

    folk elements: _____

17. When was the first rock musical written? _____

    What was it? _____

    What are some others? _____

    _____

18. List three shows that you have seen (on stage or on video).
    Name the composer and lyricist, if you know them.

    a. _____

    b. _____

    c. _____

19. New musicals have been written on such literary classics as *Les Misérables* and *The Phantom of the Opera*. Suggest a book that you think would be adaptable to the musical theater stage, and tell why you believe it could succeed.

    _____

    _____

    _____

    _____

    _____

    _____

> **90. *Listening* Rodgers/Hart and Bernstein**
> Rodgers: *My Funny Valentine,* * original version (**LG** 69 C/S)
> jazz version (**LG** 69 C/S; 35 Sh)
> Bernstein: Symphonic Dances from *West Side Story,* excerpts (**LG** 70 C/S; 36 Sh)

*Listen to *My Funny Valentine* in its original version, from Rodgers and Hart's *Babes in Arms.* Answer the questions below.

1. What is the setting for the 1937 show *Babes in Arms?*

2. Who sings *My Funny Valentine* in the show? _____

3. What determines the **A-B-A′** structure of the refrain of the song?

4. How does the singing style of the verse differ from the refrain?

5. Who wrote the text to this song? _____

6. Why do you suppose the verse is written in archaic English?

7. Did you know this song before studying it here? _____

   If yes, from where? _____

Listen to the jazz version of this song as performed by the Gerry Mulligan Quartet. Answer the questions below.

8. What is the instrumentation of the quartet? _____

9. What instruments are featured in solos? _____

10. What changes does this jazz version make in the form of the song?

11. Describe the mood of this performance. _____

12. What characteristics of West Coast jazz do you hear?

Listen to the excerpts from Bernstein's Symphonic Dances from *West Side Story*, and answer the questions below.

13. Who wrote the lyrics to *West Side Story*? _____

14. What is the story about? _____

    _____

15. Which songs from the musical do you hear in these excerpts from the Symphonic Dances? _____

16. What sounds jazzlike about these dance scenes? _____

    _____

17. What gives the music a Latin-American flavor? _____

    _____

18. When does the "Rumble" dance episode occur in the story?

    _____

    _____

19. How does the music evoke the images of the "Rumble" scene?

    _____

    _____

20. How are the music and story of *West Side Story* still relevant today?

    _____

    _____

21. Is Bernstein a classical (art) or popular composer? Explain your response.

    _____

    _____

22. In addition to composing, what other musical roles did Bernstein fill during his lifetime? _____

    _____

91. *Exploring* Latin-American Dance Music
(**CP** 23 C/Sh/S)

Complete the following questions.

1. Name some Latin-American dances that have become popular in Europe and America, and identify their country of origin.

_____

_____

_____

_____

2. What are the two meanings of the word "conga"? _____

_____

_____

3. To what musical style does the term "salsa" refer? _____

_____

_____

What does the term mean literally? _____

4. Where did ska and reggae originate? _____

Describe the musical style of ska. _____

_____

_____

Which pop song introduced the style into the United States?

_____

5. Describe the musical characteristics of reggae. _____

_____

_____

6. What is world beat? _____

_____

_____

Music listening assignment: Select either A or B below.

    A. Listen to a recording of calypso music (a style from Trinidad, often associated with Carnival celebrations). Answer the questions below regarding the musical style. (A well-known example appears in the movie *Beetlejuice*, with a famous calypso sung by Harry Belafonte.)

    B. Listen to a recording of reggae music (Bob Marley and the Wailers or any other group), and answer the questions below regarding the musical style.

Selection: _____

Group/Performer: _____

Melodic and rhythmic characteristics: _____

_____

_____

_____

Harmonic and formal characteristics: _____

_____

_____

Instruments used: _____

_____

_____

_____

Subject of text: _____

_____

_____

Comments: _____

_____

_____

_____

---

92. *Reviewing* A History of Rock
(Chap. 75 C/S; 67 Sh)

Answer the following questions.

1. What is rhythm and blues? _____

   _____

   Name several performers in this style. _____

   _____

2. What other styles of music contributed to the development of rock and

   roll? _____

3. Name two African-American and two white rock and roll stars from the

   1950s.

   African American: _____

   White: _____

4. Describe briefly each of the following popular styles, and name at least
   one performer or group associated with each.

   a. Soft rock: _____

      Group: _____

   b. Acid rock: _____

      Group: _____

   c. Art rock: _____

      Group: _____

   d. Heavy metal: _____

      Group: _____

   e. Punk rock: _____

      Group: _____

   f. Reggae: _____

      Group: _____

   g. Rap: _____

      Group: _____

   h. Grunge rock: _____

      Group: _____

5. Why are the Beatles so important to the history of rock?

_____

_____

_____

What accounts for their current revival? _____

_____

6. How have rock videos and MTV changed the way we listen to and judge

popular music? _____

_____

_____

_____

7. What other technological developments have revolutionized rock?

_____

_____

_____

8. What two groups or performers from the 1980s do you think were most

influential to the development of rock? _____

_____

9. What groups that are currently popular do you think will be

remembered ten years from now? _____

_____

_____

---

93. *Listening* Rock and the Global Scene
 *Dylan: *Mr. Tambourine Man* by the Byrds (**LG** 71 C/S)
 Black Magic Woman/Gypsy Queen by Santana (**LG** 72 C/S; 37 Sh)
 That's Why I Choose You by Ladysmith Black Mambazo (**LG** 73 C/S; 38 Sh)

---

*Listen to *Mr. Tambourine Man* as sung by the Byrds, and answer the questions below.

1. What style of rock does this song represent? _____

2. What famous protest singer wrote and first recorded this song?

   _____

3. Describe the vocal style heard in this song. _____

   _____

4. What do you think this song is about? _____

   _____

   _____

5. What was innovative about the instruments used in this recording?

   _____

6. Why do you think this recording achieved great popularity in the mid
   1960s?_____

   _____

7. What other tunes did the Byrds make famous? _____

   _____

Listen to the recording of *Black Magic Woman/Gypsy Queen* as performed by
Santana, and answer the following.

8. Who wrote the music and text for *Black Magic Woman?* _____

   With what group did he perform?_____

9. Who wrote the music for *Gypsy Queen?* _____

10. What style of rock does this song represent? _____

    What musical characteristics of this style are heard here?

    _____

11. Which instruments are featured in solos in this performance?

    _____

12. For what other styles of music is Carlos Santana known?

_____

13. Have you heard this group before? _____ this song?_____

14. How do you account for the continued popularity of Santana?

_____

_____

Listen to the Ladysmith Black Mambazo performance of *That's Why I Choose You*, and respond below.

15. What type of ensemble is this? _____

What role does Joseph Shabalala play? _____

16. Describe the singing style heard in this song. _____

_____

_____

17. What elements of this style have traditional African roots?

_____

_____

What African tribe developed this style?_____

18. What sounds Western about this song? _____

_____

19. How long has this particular style been popular in the West?

_____ What group and song introduced it?

_____

20. How did Paul Simon help promote the music of South Africa?

_____

_____

94. *Exploring* The Sounds of World Beat
(**CP** 24 C/Sh/S)

Complete the following questions.

1. Name some contemporary performing groups that represent world beat (or ethno-pop) music and their country of origin.

_____

_____

_____

2. What accounts for the current global trend in popular music?

_____

_____

_____

_____

3. How did Woodstock (1969) broaden awareness of world musics?

_____

_____

_____

4. Are world beat recordings representative of an authentic traditional style? _____

Why are field recordings considered authentic? _____

_____

_____

_____

5. Explain how different styles are combined in world beat music.

_____

_____

_____

_____

Music listening assignment: Listen to a recording of a world beat group (such as The Chieftains, the Gyōtō monks, the Mahotella Queens, Youssou N'Dour, or selections from Paul Simon's *Graceland* album), and describe its musical style below.

Group/Performer: _____

Medium (voices/instruments): _____

Selection: _____

What elements of the style are drawn from popular music?

_____

_____

_____

_____

_____

What elements are drawn from traditional, or folk, music?

_____

_____

_____

_____

_____

What elements are drawn from art music (if any)?

_____

_____

What instruments are used (if any)?

_____

_____

Comments: _____

_____

_____

---

95. *Reviewing* **The New Music**
(Chap. 76–77 C/S; 68–69 Sh)

Complete the following questions.

1. Name an artist associated with each of the following trends.

    a. Pop Art: _____

    b. Post-Modernism: _____

    c. Abstract Expressionism: _____

    d. New-wave cinema: _____

    e. Performance art: _____

2. Cite some types of recent experiments that have taken place in the
following genres.

    a. Poetry: _____

    _____

    b. Theater: _____

    _____

    c. Cinema: _____

    _____

3. How has the feminist movement affected recent developments in the

    arts? _____

    _____

True or False

____ 4. Total serialism is an extension of twelve-tone music to include the
complex organization of other musical elements.

____ 5. Aleatoric music referred to an ultrarational, total serial music.

____ 6. Open form is a flexible structure related to aleatoric music.

____ 7. John Cage was associated with aleatoric music.

____ 8. The piano is not capable of playing microtones, as they fall between
its notes.

Match the following contemporary composers with their native countries (you may use an answer more than once).

_____ 9. Pierre Boulez   a. Greece

_____ 10. Luciano Berio   b. Russia

_____ 11. Iannis Xenakis   c. United States

_____ 12. Krzysztof Penderecki   d. France

_____ 13. George Perle   e. Italy

_____ 14. Sophia Gubaidulina   f. Poland

_____ 15. Elliott Carter

_____ 16. Witold Lutosławski

_____ 17. John Cage

18. What is a prepared piano? _____

_____

19. What is the point of a work with no musical content, such as Cage's
4′33″ ?

_____

_____

_____

20. Name four female virtuoso singers who have specialized in
contemporary music.

a. _____   b. _____

c. _____   d. _____

21. The role of women in music, and especially as composers, has changed
radically over the centuries. What general perception do you have of
the role of women in music today?

_____

_____

_____

_____

_____

---

96. *Exploring* Canada's Vision for a Global Culture
(**CP** 25 C/Sh/S)

Complete the following questions.

1. What cultures make up Canada's multi-ethnic population?

   _____

   _____

2. Describe Canada's commitment to avant-garde music. _____

   _____

   _____

   _____

   _____

   _____

3. Which contemporary Canadian writer was influential to modern

   composers? _____

   Describe his philosophy about communication in the twentieth century.

   _____

   _____

   _____

   _____

4. What is the goal of composer R. Murray Schafer's World Soundscapes

   project? _____

   _____

   _____

5. How has Schafer changed music performance conventions?

   _____

   _____

   _____

Music listening assignment. Investigate a multimedia or performance art work by one of the composers listed below. Read about the work, listen to it (if possible), and discuss how it changes standard conventions of performance.

Laurie Anderson
John Cage
Pauline Oliveros
R. Murray Schafer

Work: _____ Date: _____

Composer: _____

Medium (performance forces): _____

_____

Description of work: _____

_____

_____

_____

_____

How is this different from standard performance ritual?

_____

_____

_____

_____

_____

_____

_____

Comments: _____

_____

_____

_____

---

97. *Listening* Carter, Boulez, and Lutosławski*
*Carter: Sonata for Flute, Oboe, Cello, and Harpsichord, First Movement
  (**LG** 74 C/S)
*Boulez: *The Hammer Without a Master*, Nos. 1, 3, 7 (**LG** 75 C/S)
*Lutosławski: *Venetian Games*, First Movement (**LG** 76 C/S)

---

*Listen to the first movement of the Carter sonata, and answer the following questions.

1. Who commissioned this work? _____

2. What is unusual about the instrumentation of the sonata?

   _____

   What is the composer's explanation for his choice of instruments?

   _____

3. How would you describe the tempo and metric treatment in this

   movement? _____

4. Is it easy to follow the melodic line throughout? _____

   Explain. _____

   _____

5. In what other musical genres does Carter write? _____

   _____

6. For which pieces was he honored with prestigious awards?

   _____

   _____

*Listen to the three movements from Boulez's *Hammer Without a Master*, and respond below.

7. What is the medium for this chamber work? _____

   _____

8. Who is the poet? _____ What is the text of No. 3

   about? _____

9. How does Boulez achieve some effects from non-Western music?

   _____

   _____

193

10. How would you describe the harmonic style? _____

11. What unifies this song cycle? _____

12. Describe the style of the vocal line. _____

_____

13. What important musical positions has Pierre Boulez held?

_____

*Listen to the first movement from Lutosławski's *Venetian Games,* and respond below.

14. For what occasion was this work written? _____

_____

15. What does it mean that some sections are aleatoric?

_____

Which sections are aleatoric? _____

What sections are fully notated? _____

_____

16. Can you tell these sections apart by listening? _____

17. How does the composer use timbre (or instrumental color) to shape the work? _____

_____

18. Describe your reaction to this work. _____

_____

_____

---

98. *Listening* Crumb and Ligeti

Crumb: *Ancient Voices of Children*, First Movement (**LG** 77 C/S; 39 Sh)
Ligeti: *Disorder*, from Etudes for Piano, Book I (**LG** 78 C/S; 40 Sh)

Listen to *The Little Boy Is Looking for His Voice*, from Crumb's *Ancient Voices of Children*, and respond below.

1. Whose poetry is set in this song cycle? _____

   Describe the poet. _____

2. What other works did Crumb set to texts by the same poet?

   _____

3. Why was Crumb so attracted to this poet's writings? _____

   _____

4. What is unusual about the instruments used in this work?

   _____

   _____

5. What unusual effects is the voice asked to reproduce?

   _____

   _____

6. Describe the vocalise singing style that opens this song:

   _____

   _____

7. Can you hear when the text is finally sung? _____

8. Who sings the second strophe of the song? _____

   What is unusual about the way this is sung? _____

   _____ Can you hear this strophe? _____

9. What non-Western styles are suggested in this song? _____

   _____

10. What extraordinary singer recorded this work? _____

Listen to Ligeti's *Disorder,* from his Etudes for Piano, Book I, and respond below.

11. What were some of the influences on Ligeti in writing these études?

    _____

    _____

12. What element is manipulated the most in this work? _____

13. Would you describe the work as unstructured or highly structured?

    _____

    Explain. _____

    _____

14. Why is the title *Disorder* appropriate for this work?

    _____

    _____

15. How would you describe the character of this piano work?

    _____

16. How does the étude end? _____

    _____

17. How demanding do you think this work is to perform?

    _____

18. What famous film made use of Ligeti's music? _____

    What works were included in this soundtrack? _____

    _____

    Have you seen this film? _____

    When was it made? _____

    Who was the film's director? _____

---

99. *Reviewing* Technology and Music
(Chap. 79 C/S; 70 Sh)

Complete the following.

1. _____ is a French term describing music made up of natural sounds that were recorded and manipulated.

2. What is a synthesizer? _____

   _____

3. Who are some important composers in the field of electronic music?

   _____

4. Describe the early electronic work *Poème électronique.*

   _____

   _____

   _____

5. What is Milton's Babbitt's philosophy concerning music and the

   listener? _____

   _____

   What attracted Babbitt to the medium of electronic music?

   _____

*6. Babbitt's work *Phonemena* exists in two versions, with differing accompaniments. What are they?

   _____

   For whom and what occasion did he write *Phonemena?* _____

   _____

   What is a phoneme? _____

   How many phonemes are there? _____

*7. Do you think this work would have been more or less effective with

   intelligible words? _____ Explain.

   _____

8. How does Tod Machover use computers in his music? _____

   _____

   _____

9. What is a hyper-instrument? _____

_____

_____

10. What is the purpose of the electronic glove devised by Machover?

_____

_____

11. What does Machover's title *Bug-Mudra* mean? _____

_____

_____

12. What kind of instruments are used in this work? _____

_____

_____

13. How do performers interact with the computer in this work?

_____

_____

14. Describe your reaction to *Bug-Mudra* after listening to this excerpt.

_____

_____

_____

_____

---

100. *Exploring* **Music and the World of Technology**
(**CP** 26 C/Sh/S)

Complete the following questions.

1. How does commercial music make use of new technologies?

2. What is MIDI, and how has this technology revolutionized music?

3. How is the computer used as a tool by composers? _____

4. How can the computer be used in live performances?

5. What is CD-ROM technology, and how do we interact with it?

6. What is the Internet? _____

Music listening assignment: Listen to a popular music recording by a group of your choice. Describe the group's instrumentation, and what elements of the style and recording were made possible through technology.

Selection: _____

Group: _____

To what extent is the group's instrumentation electrified?

_____

_____

_____

To what extent does the group use synthesizers or drum machine?

_____

_____

_____

_____

What studio techniques do you think were used to manipulate music

in this recording? _____

_____

_____

_____

_____

Comments: _____

_____

_____

_____

_____

_____

---

101. *Listening* **New Romanticism and Minimalism**

Tower: *Petroushskates*(**LG** 81 C/S; 42 Sh)

*Adams: *Nixon in China,* Act I, Scene 3, Finale (**LG** 82 C/S)

Multiple Choice

_____ 1. Which is most typical of the aspirations of composers of the New Romanticism?
   a. purely intellectual, completely serial composition
   b. music as "the language of the emotions"
   c. formal, constructivist art

_____ 2. The New Romantics sought to:
   a. close the gap between composers and listeners.
   b. further widen the gap between composers and listeners.
   c. follow the harmonic and melodic language of the Baroque.

_____ 3. Which term best describes the marked stylistic feature of minimalist music?
   a. dissonance
   b. repetition
   c. contrast

_____ 4. What was the primary impetus for minimalist composers?
   a. a return to simplicity
   b. a total abandonment of form
   c. a desire for overstatement

Complete the following questions.

5. Name three composers who are advocates of the New Romanticism.

   a. _____

   b. _____

   c. _____

6. Name three composers who have turned to writing minimalist music.

   a. _____

   b. _____

   c. _____

7. How would you describe the effect that minimalist music has on the

   listener? _____

   _____

Listen to Tower's chamber work *Petroushskates,* and respond below.

8. What is the instrumentation for the work? _____

_____

9. What composer and work does Tower parody in this composition?

_____

    Where do you hear this borrowing? _____

    What other idea inspired this work? _____

    What instruments present this idea? _____

10. What other composer has Tower parodied? _____

*Listen to the excerpt from John Adams's opera *Nixon in China,* and answer the following questions.

11. On which historical event is this opera based?_____

_____

12. With whom did Adams collaborate to produce this opera?

_____

13. Which more recent event is the subject of another Adams opera?

_____

14. Describe the vocal style heard in Nixon's speech. _____

_____

15. What gives this work its propelling energy? _____

_____

16. Which style do you think will be longer lasting: New Romanticism or minimalism? _____

    Why? _____

_____

_____

102. *Exploring* The Non-Western Roots of Minimalism and New-Age Music (CP 27 C/Sh/S)

Complete the following questions.

1. To what extent did nineteenth-century composers study foreign

cultures and music? _____

_____

_____

How have contemporary composers studied world musics?_____

_____

_____

2. In which music cultures was composer Steve Reich interested?

_____

What attracted him to these styles? _____

_____

3. Where and what did Reich study before writing his work *Drumming*?

_____

_____

4. What do audiences find attractive about minimalist music?

_____

_____

5. How has minimalist music influenced rock? _____

_____

_____

How has it influenced new-age music? _____

_____

_____

6. Name several new-age recording artists. _____

_____

Music listening assignment: Select either A or B below.

A. Listen to a minimalist work by Steve Reich, Terry Riley, or Philip Glass. Describe below its primary musical characteristics (melody, rhythm, harmony, texture, form, timbre, instruments). (You should be able to find recordings by these composers in your library.)

B. Listen to an example of African drumming (preferably from Ghana). Describe below its primary musical characteristics, focusing on its rhythm and meter, texture, and instruments. (Look for a recording in your library, or ask your instructor to provide one from the Music Example Bank.)

Selection: _____

Composer/Country: _____

_____

_____

_____

_____

_____

_____

_____

_____

_____

_____

_____

_____

_____

_____

_____

_____

_____

_____

_____

_____

---

103. *Reviewing* **Musical Notation**
(Appendix I)

Answer the following questions about the musical example below. The piece is a Jamaican folk song entitled *Matilda*.

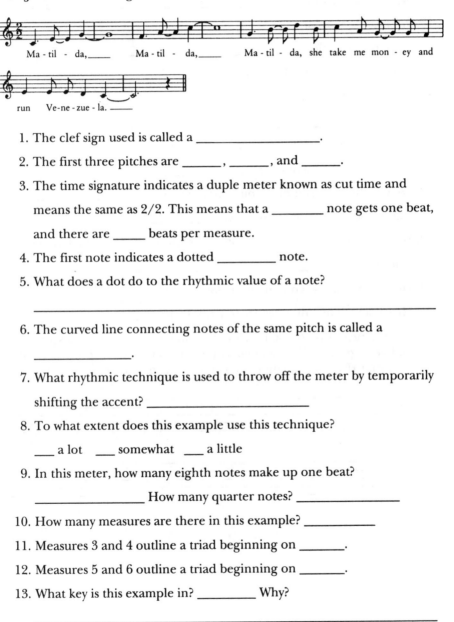

Ma - til - da, ____   Ma - til - da, ____   Ma - til - da, she take me mon - ey and

run   Ve - ne - zue - la. ____

1. The clef sign used is called a _____.

2. The first three pitches are _____, _____, and _____.

3. The time signature indicates a duple meter known as cut time and

    means the same as 2/2. This means that a _____ note gets one beat,

    and there are _____ beats per measure.

4. The first note indicates a dotted _____ note.

5. What does a dot do to the rhythmic value of a note?

    _____

6. The curved line connecting notes of the same pitch is called a

    _____.

7. What rhythmic technique is used to throw off the meter by temporarily

    shifting the accent? _____

8. To what extent does this example use this technique?

    ___ a lot   ___ somewhat   ___ a little

9. In this meter, how many eighth notes make up one beat?

    _____ How many quarter notes? _____

10. How many measures are there in this example? _____

11. Measures 3 and 4 outline a triad beginning on _____.

12. Measures 5 and 6 outline a triad beginning on _____.

13. What key is this example in? _____ Why?

    _____

14. Name a song you know that begins with an upbeat.

_____

15. Name a song you know that is in triple meter.

_____

16. What is the sign for a sharp? _____

What is its function? _____

17. What is the sign for a flat? _____

What is its function? _____

18. How do you cancel a flat or sharp? _____

19. What is the function of a key signature? _____

_____

20. Does the song *Matilda* have a key signature? _____

21. How do you show a quarter note rest? _____

22. What is the most common compound meter? _____

Name a song in compound meter. _____

23. What do you call short lines above or below the staff on which notes are written? _____

24. How many thirty-second notes make up a half note? _____

25. How many sixteenth notes are in a whole note? _____

26. Write a melody on the staff below, beginning with a clef, time signature, and key signature. You can make up the pitches and rhythms, but make sure your rhythmic notation is correct for each measure.

Workbook Activity Assignments

The following exercises allow you to explore various types of music on your own or with a small group (a study or discussion group, for example). They are designed to make you more aware of the diverse opportunities you have to hear music, and of ways in which you can actively participate in making music. They can also guide you in doing special projects or in completing work assigned by your instructor. There are, of course, many variations that are possible with these activities; if you have ideas for different projects, talk them over with your instructor.

1. Music Journal
2. Interview with a Musician
3. Interview with an International Student
4. An International Night Out
5. Exploring PBS Programming
6. Viewing Opera from Home
7. Exploring MTV
8. Reliving Woodstock (1969)
9. Karaoke Singing
10. Group Singing
11. Writing a Rap Song
12. Percussion Ensemble

Activity 1: Music Journal

Goal: To become more aware of music in your environment.

Instructions: Keep a journal in the space below for four days, noting all the instances in which you listen to or hear music (whether by your own choosing or by accident). Consider the following: your clock radio, car and/or home stereo, television (even as background music), music at work, in class, in stores, and in elevators.

DAY 1   Date _____

AM: _____

_____

_____

_____

PM: _____

_____

_____

_____

DAY 2   Date _____

AM: _____

_____

_____

PM: _____

_____

_____

_____

DAY 3   Date _____

AM: _____

_____

_____

_____

PM: _____

_____

_____

_____

_____

DAY 4   Date _____

AM: _____

_____

_____

PM: _____

_____

_____

_____

_____

Were you surprised how often (or seldom) you heard music?

_____

Were you more aware than usual of music in your environment? _____

Was any of the music distracting or annoying? _____

Comments: _____

_____

_____

_____

_____

Activity 2: Interview with a Musician

Goal: To gain insight into musical performance from an active participant.

Instructions: Find a musician or conductor on campus (a music student or instructor), and arrange an interview. Ask him or her the questions below, along with others that you supply.

Interview Questions

What is your name? _____

Are you ____ a performer, ____ a conductor, or ____ both?

How long have you studied music? _____

What instrument(s) do you play? _____

Do you sing? _____ If yes, what voice range? _____

In which music ensembles have you participated and in what capacity?

_____

_____

_____

Do you take part in concerts frequently? _____

Approximately how many performances a year? _____

Describe a recent performance in which you participated (group, which instrument/voice, and repertory performed).

_____

_____

_____

_____

_____

How is active participation in music making different from passive listening?

_____

_____

_____

_____

What decisions must you make while performing music?

_____

_____

_____

_____

What styles of music do you most often perform?

____ classical   ____ popular   ____ traditional

Describe the specific styles you perform frequently.

_____

_____

Do you now (or plan to) make your living as a musician? ____ yes ____ no

Comments: _____

What are the advantages of a career in music? _____

_____

_____

What are the disadvantages? _____

_____

_____

(Your comments here): _____

_____

_____

_____

_____

Activity 3: Interview with an International Student

Goal: To learn about the music of another culture from a native.

Instructions: Find an international student (or instructor) on your campus. (Ask in your classes, post a note on a dorm or student union bulletin board, or go to the International Office on your campus.) Arrange to meet with this person, and ask him or her the questions below, along with others that you supply.

Interview Questions

What is your name? _____

What country do you come from? _____

What is your native language? _____

How long have you been in this country? _____

What are you studying here? _____

Have you ever studied music? _____

Do you play any instruments? _____ If yes, which one(s)?

_____

Did you learn any native folk songs as a child? _____

Can you sing one or tell me about one?

Title: _____ Language: _____

What is it about? _____

_____

_____

(Make your own notes about the song below.)

_____

_____

What kind of instruments are used in your native folk music?

_____

What roles does music play in your society? _____

_____

Do women study music there? If so, what kind? _____

_____

Do men study music there? If so, what kind? _____

_____

What kind of music do you like to listen to? _____

_____

Do you plan to take any music classes while studying here? _____

If yes, which? _____

Have you been to any concerts in this country? _____

If yes, which? _____

_____

Is popular music in your country influenced by American popular styles?

_____ If yes, in what way? _____

_____

(Note other questions you asked below, with the answers, or any comments
you have about the interview.)

_____

_____

_____

_____

_____

_____

_____

_____

_____

Activity 4: An International Night Out

Goal: To hear live music from another culture, in either a concert or restaurant setting.

Instructions:
   A. Attend a concert on campus or in the community by a non-Western or traditional music group (solo performer, choral, instrumental, or dance group); or
   B. Go to an international restaurant that features authentic live music.

Complete the questions below.

Date of event: _____ Place: _____

Was this a _____ concert or _____ restaurant entertainment?

Names of performers: _____

_____

Country or culture of origin: _____

Did you hear singing? ____ yes ____ no

If yes, describe the style you heard. _____

_____

Did you hear instruments? ____ yes ____ no

If yes, which instruments? _____

_____

Did you see dancing? ____ yes ____ no

If yes, what style of dancing was it? _____

_____

Were the performers in native costume? ____ yes ____ no

If yes, describe them. _____

_____

Do you know the titles of any works performed? ____ yes ____ no

If yes, list some. _____

_____

_____

Describe the music you heard in your own words (consider the melody, rhythm, harmony, and texture).

_____

_____

_____

_____

_____

_____

_____

Did you like the music? _____ yes _____ no

Why or why not? _____

_____

If you attended a restaurant, did you eat ethnic food? _____ yes _____ no

If yes, what kinds? _____

_____

Did you like the food? _____ yes _____ no

Is this the first time you have heard live music of this style?

_____ yes _____ no

Would you go to another concert/restaurant entertainment of the same type?

_____ yes _____ no

Activity 5: Exploring PBS Programming

Goal: To become aware of the diverse music programs and live performances available on PBS (Public Broadcasting System).

Instructions: Determine which TV station in your area is affiliated with the Public Broadcasting System, and review the programming for a week. Choose a music program (any style), watch it, and discuss it below.

Progam title: _____

Station: _____ Date/time of program: _____

Major performers/groups: _____

_____

_____

Titles of selected works (if known): _____

_____

_____

What type of music was performed?

___ classical If yes, what eras? _____

___ popular If yes, what styles? _____

___ traditional If yes, what styles? _____

___ non-Western If yes, what styles? _____

If dramatic music, was it an ___ opera ___ ballet ___ musical ___ other?

List other music programs offered during the week. _____

_____

_____

_____

_____

_____

_____

Describe the performance in your own words. Try to mention some elements of musical style, and evaluate the performance.

_____

_____

_____

_____

_____

_____

_____

_____

_____

_____

_____

_____

_____

Did you enjoy the program? ___ yes ___ no ___ somewhat

Would you have enjoyed it ___ more ___ less ___the same, if you had been at the live concert?

Comments: _____

_____

_____

_____

_____

Activity 6: Viewing Opera from Home

Goal: To become familiar with an opera of your choice and its characteristic traits.

Instructions: Go to your local video store (or campus or public library), select an opera video that interests you, watch it, and discuss it below.

Opera title: _____

Composer: _____

When was the opera written (check your text)? _____

In what language is it sung? _____

Does the video have English subtitles? _____ yes _____ no

Which opera company performed? _____

Name the leading solo performers (check credits or box).

_____

_____

_____

Who are the main characters in the opera? _____

_____

_____

_____

Summarize the plot below. _____

_____

_____

_____

_____

_____

_____

_____

_____

_____

_____

_____

_____

_____

_____

_____

_____

_____

Was this ___ comic or ____ serious opera?

Did it begin with an instrumental overture? ____ yes ___ no

Check below the vocal styles that you heard.

___ aria ___ recitative ___ solo ensemble ___ chorus

Describe the music in your own words. _____

_____

_____

_____

_____

_____

Did you enjoy the opera? ___ yes ___ no ___ somewhat

Would you like to see another? ___ yes ___ no

If yes, ___ on video or ___ in live performance?

Comments: _____

_____

_____

_____

_____

Activity 7: Exploring MTV
(Chap. 7–9 C/Sh/S)

Goal: To assess the programming on MTV (Music Television) and the impact the network has had on popular music.

Instructions: Review MTV programming for two or three days. Choose several diverse music programs to watch, and answer the following questions.

Program (1) title: _____

Date: _____ Time: _____ Program length: _____

Program (2) title: _____

Date: _____ Time: _____ Program length: _____

List some of the other programs offered that you did not select.

_____

_____

_____

Describe program 1 (groups performing, focus or theme).

_____

_____

_____

_____

_____

What styles of popular music were included?

___ soft rock	___ punk rock
___ folk rock	___ reggae
___ jazz rock	___ rap
___ art rock	___ grunge rock
___ Latin rock	___ new wave
___ heavy metal	

other _____

Describe one musical style you heard and its characteristics.

_____

_____

Describe program 2 (groups performing, focus or theme).

_____

_____

_____

_____

_____

What styles of popular music were included?

___ soft rock   ___ punk rock

___ folk rock   ___ reggae

___ jazz rock   ___ rap

___ art rock   ___ grunge rock

___ Latin rock   ___ new wave

___ heavy metal

other: _____

_____

Describe one musical style you heard and its characteristics.

_____

_____

Do you watch MTV often? ___ yes ___ no ___ sometimes

Do you prefer ___ MTV or ___ listening to a CD or cassette?

Explain your answer. _____

_____

What effect do you think MTV has had on the popular music industry?

_____

_____

_____

Activity 8: Reliving Woodstock (1969)

Goal: To become familiar with various 1960s-era rock groups and styles through a historic event.

Instructions: Go to your college (or public) library or to a video store and check out the double video of Woodstock (1969). Watch parts of it, and answer the questions below.

The following are some recommended performances on the video (counter numbers and timings are provided for easy access).

TAPE 1

Counter	Time	Performer/Group	Song
1785	23:10	Richie Havens	*Freedom* (adapted from *Motherless Child*)
2708	40:00	Joan Baez	*Joe Hill* / *Swing Low, Sweet Chariot*
2965	45:25	The Who	*We're Not Gonna Take It* / *Summertime Blues*
3770	63:50	Sha-Na-Na	*At the Hop*
3978	68:40	Joe Cocker	*With a Little Help from My Friends*

TAPE 2

Counter	Time	Performer/Group	Song
0000	0:00	Country Joe/Fish	*Rock and Soul Music*
0225	3:30	Arlo Guthrie	*Comin' into Los Angeles*
0580	6:15	Crosby, Stills and Nash	*Judy Blue Eyes*
1280	15:20	Ten Years After	*I'm Going Home*
2370	25:00	John Sebastian	*Rainbows All Over Your Blues*
2664	40:50	Country Joe MacDonald	*I Feel Like I'm Fixin' to Die Rag*
3185	51:37	Santana	*Soul Sacrifice*
3597	61:07	Sly and the Family Stone	*I Want to Take You Higher*
4382	81:00	Jimi Hendrix	*The Star-Spangled Banner*

Select three performances representing different groups and styles to answer these questions.

Group (1): _____

Title (1): _____

What style rock is this? _____

Did you know the group or recording prior to this video?

___ group ___ song ___ both

Describe the musical elements of the style. _____

_____

_____

_____

Group (2): _____

Title (2):_____

What style rock is this? _____

Did you know the group or recording prior to this video?

___ group ___ song ___ both

Describe the musical elements of the style. _____

_____

_____

_____

Group (3): _____

Title (3): _____

What style rock is this? _____

Did you know the group or recording prior to this video?

___ group ___ song ___ both

Describe the musical elements of the style. _____

_____

_____

_____

Why is Woodstock remembered as a historic event? _____

_____

_____

_____

Do you think Woodstock II (1995) will be as famous an event?

_____

Activity 9.: Karaoke Singing

Goal: To be actively involved in music performance as an amateur singer.

Instructions: Find a karaoke club in your area, or check out or buy a karaoke track to use at home or in class, and perform as a solo (or group) singer. (If you are unsure what karaoke is, look it up in your text.)

Date: _____ Location: _____

List the song(s) you sang: _____

_____

_____

List songs others sang: _____

_____

_____

Did you know the words for the songs you sang? ___ yes ___ no

Did you have the words available to look at? ___ yes ___ no

If yes, did you have ___ printed text or ___ a monitor?

Did you sing ___ as a soloist or ___ with a group?

Describe how it felt to be a singer. _____

_____

_____

_____

_____

_____

Were you able to sing "in tune" (on pitch)?

___ yes ___ no ___ sometimes

Do you think you have a good singing voice? ___ yes ___ no

Did other singers sing "in tune"?

___ yes ___ no ___ sometimes

Describe how one of the other singers sounded. _____

_____

_____

Did others have good singing voices?

___ yes ___ no ___ some did

In your opinion, what determines a good voice? _____

_____

_____

_____

Where did the tradition of karaoke singing originate?

_____

What do you think accounts for its popularity? _____

_____

_____

Have you ever done this before? ___ yes ___ no

Would you enjoy trying it again? ___ yes ___ no

Comments: _____

_____

_____

_____

Activity 10: Group Singing

Goal: To study imitation through the singing of a round.

Instructions: The song below is a famous round titled *Sumer is icumen in*, or the *Summer* Canon. The song is in Medieval English and dates from the thirteenth century. It has a melody that can be sung as a four-voice round, and two lower voices, each an ostinato (called a *pes*, pronounced "pace").

Practice singing the melody line together, then learn the two lower parts. To sing as a round, divide into melody singers (four groups; two or three groups are also possible) and ostinato, or *pes*, singers (two groups). Have the two lower parts begin (they will help keep time), then have melody group 1 enter, then group 2, then 3, and finally 4 in overlapping imitation. Each group enters with the melody, starting when the previous group reaches number 2 in the music; each continues through the whole piece, repeating it as many times as needed. Remember that a round can go on indefinitely, so decide how many times you will sing the work.

Note that the lower parts are notated in the bass clef. (*Performance note:* The music is transposed to C major. A score of the resulting piece is on the next page. Instruments may be used instead of voices on any parts.)

Poem	*Translation (modern English)*
Sing cuccu; sing cuccu, nu	Sing, cuckoo; sing cuckoo, now
Sing cuccu, nu sing cuccu!	Sing, cuckoo, now sing, cuckoo!
Sumer is icumen in,	Summer is coming on,
Lhude sing cuccu!	Loudly sing, cuckoo!
Groweth sed and bloweth med,	The seeds are growing and the meadow is blooming,
And springth the wde nu	And the woods are budding.
Sing cuccu!	Sing, cuckoo!
Awe bleteth after lomb,	The ewe bleats for the lamb,
Lhouth after calve cu;	The cow lows for the calf;
Bulloc sterteth,	The bullock jumps,
Bucke verteth,	The buck breaks wind,
Murie sing cuccu	Merrily sing, cuckoo.
Cuccu, cuccu,	Cuckoo, cuckoo,
Wel singes thu cuccu,	Well you sing, cuckoo,
Ne swik thu naver nu.	Do not ever stop now.

Melody and 2 short *pes* (ostinato) parts:

Resulting music when sung as a round, showing imitation of lines:

Activity 11: Writing a Rap Song

Goal: To understand what musical elements make up rap, and to recreate the style.

Instructions: Create a rap song of your own composition. Since rap is a combination of rhymed lyrics spoken or recited over a rhythm track, you have two different tasks:

1. Create a rhythm track with a steady beat. You can do this in one of four ways:
   a. record simple rhythmic patterns you make up and play;
   b. produce a "sample" from sounds and older prerecorded pieces;
   c. use a prerecorded rhythm setting on an electronic keyboard or drum machine; or
   d. buy a rap rhythm track in a music store.

If you write your own rhythmic accompaniment, it can be very simple. Think in terms of long (L) and short (S) durations, and make it in quadruple meter. Here is an example that should be counted in 4 at a quick pace (notice it begins with an upbeat):

SSL SL SSL SL SSL SL
4 1 2 3 4 1 2 3 4 1 2 3

2. Write a text (usually rhymed) to recite over the accompanying track. Write about some current issue (political, social, or environmental).

Do you listen to rap? ___ yes ___ no ___ sometimes

Which groups are you familiar with? _____

_____

_____

_____

What is the subject matter of the rap songs you know? _____

_____

_____

_____

_____

Describe how you created a rhythm track for your song.

_____

_____

_____

_____

_____

_____

Write your song text in the space below.

_____

_____

_____

_____

_____

_____

_____

_____

_____

What do you like (or dislike) about rap from a musical point of view?

_____

_____

_____

_____

Activity 12: Percussion Ensemble

Goal: To understand polyrhythm through the spontaneous creation of a group rhythmic work.

Instructions: Work with a small group of students (three to six), with each providing a percussion instrument of his or her choice. (This could be anything that produces either a definite or indefinite pitch, and ideally, they should have differing timbres.)

1. Choose a master percussionist (or leader) to give signals to play and stop.

2. Choose a number to determine the overall cycle (the example below is based on 12). Have each player determine a different pattern to play within that cycle (as in additive meters). Be sure to keep a steady beat throughout.

```
Player 1   1 2 3 4 5 6 7 8 9 10 11 12
           X   X   X X   X   X      X

Player 2   1 2 3 4 5 6 7 8 9 10 11 12
           X X   X X   X X   X  X

Player 3   1 2 3 4 5 6 7 8 9 10 11 12
           X     X     X     X

Player 4   1 2 3 4 5 6 7 8 9 10 11 12
           X X X   X X X   X X  X
```

3. Play the piece, allowing one instrument to start, then adding others. You may wish to have one player count out loud. As it builds to a climax, players may decide to improvise on their patterns. Watch the master percussionist for a cue to stop. Try this several times until you are satisfied with the result, then try other patterns.

List the percussion instruments used below.

Player 1: _____

Player 2: _____

Player 3: _____

Player 4: _____

Player 5: _____

Player 6: _____

Who was designated the master percussionist? _____

4. Make a musical score by aligning the different beat patterns chosen by the performers (the grid below allows for patterns of up to 19 beats).

Player
```
1 __|__|__|__|__|__|__|__|__|__|__|__|__|__|__|__|__|__|__|
2 __|__|__|__|__|__|__|__|__|__|__|__|__|__|__|__|__|__|__|
3 __|__|__|__|__|__|__|__|__|__|__|__|__|__|__|__|__|__|__|
4 __|__|__|__|__|__|__|__|__|__|__|__|__|__|__|__|__|__|__|
5 __|__|__|__|__|__|__|__|__|__|__|__|__|__|__|__|__|__|__|
6 __|__|__|__|__|__|__|__|__|__|__|__|__|__|__|__|__|__|__|
   1  2  3  4  5  6  7  8  9 10 11 12 13 14 15 16 17 18 19
```

Were players successful at keeping a steady beat?

____ yes ____ no ____ somewhat

What were the difficulties in the performance? _____

_____

_____

_____

Did players freely improvise during the performance?

____ yes ____ no ____ some did

Describe how you achieved polyrhythm in your composition.

_____

_____

_____

Evaluate your musical efforts. _____

_____

_____

_____

Concert Reports

The following section is designed to guide you in knowing what to listen for at concerts and how to write a concert report. Prior to any concerts, be sure to read Appendix IV in your text, "Attending Concerts." This will help you understand traditional concert etiquette and know what to expect. It will also assist you in finding interesting programs on your campus or in the community.

There are five concert report outlines in this section, each designed for a particular type of program. The questions vary slightly, depending on whether the works are vocal or instrumental, popular or world music. The forms ask that you focus your attention on two selections (or sometimes one) to describe in some detail. Some concerts offer a mixture of styles and genres; in these cases, use either report form 1 or 2 (or ask your instructor for advice). The forms provided are for the following.

1. Instrumental music (for orchestras, bands, chamber music, or solo recitals)
2. Choral/Vocal music (for choirs, choruses, chamber choirs, and solo vocalists)
3. Dramatic music (for operas, musicals, and plays with music)
4. Popular music (for rock and jazz groups or soloists)
5. World music (for traditional and non-Western groups or soloists)

This section begins with a sample outline and report, based on the program below. These are meant as guidelines in approaching your assignment (or special project). Your instructor may ask you to submit a written report only, in which case the outline form can be used for your own notes. Take this form with you to the concert, if possible. Other instructors may wish to have only the completed outline, and some will want both the report form and a prose report. Most instructors will ask to see a copy of the concert program, and some will require that you attach the canceled ticket stub. Be sure to get clear instructions from your own instructor before completing any assignment.

PROGRAM

Overture to *A Midsummer Night's Dream*

Felix Mendelssohn
(1809–1847)

Symphony No. 40 in G minor, K. 550
  (*Jupiter*)
    Allegro vivace
    Andante cantabile
    Menuetto (Allegretto) & Trio
    Finale (Molto allegro)

W. A. Mozart
(1756–1791)

INTERMISSION

Concerto No. 1 for Piano and Orchestra
  in B-flat minor, Op. 23
    Allegro non troppo e molto maestoso;
      Allegro con spirito
    Andante simplice; Prestissimo; Tempo I
    Allegro con fuoco

P. I. Tchaikovsky
(1840–1893)

Barbara Allen, piano

The University Symphony Orchestra
Eugene Castillo, conductor

Sample Outline   Concert Report 1: Instrumental Music

Orchestra
Band
Chamber music
Solo recital

CONCERT SETTING

Date of concert: _March 7, 1995_

Place of concert: _Carpenter Performing Arts Center_

Name of group(s) performing: _University Symphony_
Orchestra, Eugene Castillo, conductor

Describe briefly the concert setting (hall, performers' dress):
the hall was large — over 1,000 seats
performers wore black (formal dress)

Were concert programs provided? _✓_ yes ___ no If yes, attach a copy.

Were program notes provided? _✓_ yes ___ no

Were there any spoken remarks about the concert? ___ yes _✓_ no

Could you follow the order of the concert? _✓_ yes ___ no

Were there any aspects of concert conventions that surprised you? _____

Which? _____

CONCERT MUSIC

Which genres of music were performed (such as symphony or sonata)?
overture, symphony, concerto

___

Did you read about any of the works performed? _✓_ yes ___no

If yes, where? _✓_ program notes ___ textbook ___ outside reading

Were any of the works programmatic (with literary or pictorial

assocations)? _✓_ yes ___ no

If yes, which? _____Overture to A Midsummer Night's Dream_____

What historical eras were represented on the program?

___ pre-1600 ___ Baroque _✓_ Classical _✓_ Romantic ___ 20th century

Choose two works from the program. Name the composer, the work, and the movement (if applicable), and compare them in the following outline:

Composer:	_Mendelssohn_	_Tchaikovsky_
Title:	_A Midsummer Night's Dream_	_Concerto No. 1 for Piano_
Movement (Section):	_opening_	_First_
Melody:	_high range and disjunct, later conjunct_	_wide range—sweeping_
Rhythm/ meter:	_duple_	_duple_
Harmony:	_consonant_	_a little dissonant_
Texture:	_homophonic_	_homophonic_
Tempo:	_Allegro (very fast)_	_Allegro (fast)_
Dynamics:	_soft at opening, then grows louder_	_loud (forte) for opening — later soft_
Instruments:	_woodwinds begin, then strings, later full orchestra_	_begins with French horns, then piano and full orchestra_
Mood:	_enchanted_	_dramatic_
Other:		

What was your overall reaction to the concert?
    ✓ enjoyed it a lot   ____ enjoyed it somewhat
    ____ did not enjoy it much   ____ did not enjoy it at all

What did you like about it? _the orchestra was all students_

What did you not like about it? _noisy students in the audience_

Other comments: _____

I attended the University Symphony Orchestra concert on Saturday night, March 7. The group was made up of student musicians and was conducted by Eugene Castillo. The pianist, Barbara Allen, is a music faculty member.

The concert hall was larger than I expected—it seated over 1,000 people, and it was nearly full. I had a good seat about halfway back in the hall. The orchestra was already on stage when I arrived. When the lights went down, the first violinist stood up and signaled the oboe player to play a note to tune the orchestra. After this, the conductor entered and began the first work, the Overture to *A Midsummer Night's Dream* by Mendelssohn, an early Romantic composer. The notes on my program explained that this was a programmatic work based on the Shakespeare play that I had read in high school. It was easy to follow the melodies for the different characters. The first theme was played by the strings in a high range, very lightly, reminding me of the fairies in the play. Later the strings played a smooth, conjunct melody that was the love theme. This was followed by a humorous, disjunct theme. All these themes returned near the end of the piece. This work was in duple meter and was mostly consonant.

The next work was a symphony by Mozart, one of his last, according to the program. It had four movements and was in a minor key. The first movement was an Allegro in sonata-allegro form. Then came a slow movement and a triple-meter minuet. The last movement was the fastest of all, with a disjunct opening melody. This work was written in the Classical era.

After the intermission, there was a piano concerto by the late Romantic Russian composer Tchaikovsky. This was a long piece, and very dramatic. The first movement had several sections. It began fast, first with the French horns, then the piano entered with disjunct chords. The strings introduced the first melody. The piano soloist played without music, and her part seemed very difficult. Her hands moved quickly as she played high and low notes on the piano. This piece was more dissonant than the other works on the program. The second movement was quiet and melancholy in mood, with a fast middle section. The last movement was in triple meter and sounded like a dance.

I enjoyed this concert very much, except for the noisy students sitting in front of me. I was impressed with how well the student musicians could play. I hope to be able to attend more concerts on campus in the future.

NAME _____ DATE _____ CLASS _____

Concert Report 1: Instrumental Music

Orchestra   ATTACH
Band   TICKET
Chamber music   STUB
Solo recital   HERE

CONCERT SETTING

Date of concert: _____

Place of concert: _____

Name of group(s) performing: _____

_____

Describe briefly the concert setting (hall, performers' dress):

_____

_____

Were concert programs provided? ___ yes ___ no If yes, attach a copy.

Were program notes provided? ___ yes ___ no

Were there any spoken remarks about the concert? ___ yes ___ no

Could you follow the order of the concert? ___ yes ___ no

Were there any aspects of concert conventions that surprised you? _____

Which? _____

CONCERT MUSIC

Which genres of music were performed (such as symphony or sonata)?

_____

_____

Did you read about any of the works performed? ___ yes ___no

If yes, where? ___ program notes ___ textbook ___ outside reading

Were any of the works programmatic (with literary or pictorial

assocations)? ___ yes ___ no

If yes, which? _____

What historical eras were represented on the program?

___ pre-1600 ___ Baroque ___ Classical ___ Romantic ___ 20th century

Choose two works from the program. Name the composer, the work, and the movement (if applicable), and compare them in the following outline:

Composer: _____   _____

Title: _____   _____

Movement
(Section): _____   _____

Melody: _____   _____
_____   _____

Rhythm/
meter: _____   _____
_____   _____

Harmony: _____   _____
_____   _____

Texture: _____   _____
_____   _____

Tempo: _____   _____
_____   _____

Dynamics: _____   _____
_____   _____

Instruments:_____   _____
_____   _____

Mood: _____   _____

Other: _____   _____

What was your overall reaction to the concert?
____ enjoyed it a lot   ____ enjoyed it somewhat
____ did not enjoy it much   ____ did not enjoy it at all

What did you like about it? _____

_____

What did you not like about it? _____

_____

Other comments: _____

_____

_____

Concert Report 2: Choral/Vocal Music

Choir/Chorus
Chamber choir/Madrigal choir
Solo vocal recital

ATTACH
TICKET
STUB
HERE

CONCERT SETTING

Date of concert: _____

Place of concert: _____

Name of group(s) performing: _____

_____

Describe briefly the group(s) performing (size, men vs. women):

_____

_____

Were concert programs provided? ___ yes ___ no If yes, attach a copy.

Were program notes provided? ___ yes ___ no

Did the program include:

the vocal texts that were sung? ___ yes ___ no

translations of foreign language texts? ___ yes ___ no

Did the concert include instrumental accompaniment? ___ yes ___ no

If yes, check those applicable ____ piano ____ organ ____ orchestra

____ harpsichord ____ small instrumental group other: _____

CONCERT MUSIC

Did the program include any of the following genres?

Choral
___ mass   ___ oratorio
___ part song ___ madrigal
___ anthem   ___ hymn
___ motet   ___ cantata

Solo vocal
___ opera aria
___ Lieder
___ song cycle

List any other genres performed. _____

_____

Did you read about any of the works performed? ___ yes ___ no

If yes, where? ___ program notes ___ textbook ___ outside reading

What historical eras were represented on the program?

___ Medieval/Renaissance   ___ Baroque   ___ Classical

___Romantic   ___ 20th century

Choose two works from the program, name the composer, the work, and the movement (if applicable) and compare them in the following outline:

Composer: _____   _____

Title: _____   _____

Movement
(Section): _____   _____

Melody: _____   _____

_____   _____

Rhythm/
meter: _____   _____

_____   _____

Harmony: _____   _____

_____   _____

Texture: _____   _____

_____   _____

Tempo: _____   _____

_____   _____

Dynamics: _____   _____

_____   _____

Instruments:_____   _____

_____   _____

Mood: _____   _____

Other: _____   _____

What was your overall reaction to the concert?

___ enjoyed it a lot   ___ enjoyed it somewhat

___ did not enjoy it much   ___ did not enjoy it at all

What did you like about it? _____

_____

What did you not like about it? _____

_____

Other comments: _____

_____

242

Concert Report 3: Dramatic Music

Opera/Operetta   ATTACH
Musical/Play with incidental music   TICKET
                                                      STUB
                                                      HERE

CONCERT SETTING

Date of concert: _____ Location: _____

Composer/Author: _____

Title of work: _____

Were concert programs provided? ___ yes ___ no If yes, attach a copy.

Were program notes provided? ___ yes ___ no

Did the program include:

the vocal texts that were sung? ___ yes ___ no

translations of foreign language texts? ___ yes ___ no

a summary of the plot or action? ___ yes ___ no

CONCERT MUSIC

In what language was the work performed? _____

In what language was it originally written? _____

Did you read about the work performed? ___ yes ___ no

If yes, where? ___ program notes ___ textbook ___ outside reading

Give a brief summary of the plot of this work.

_____

_____

_____

_____

Did the performance include instrumental accompaniment? ___ yes ___ no

If yes, was the music: ___ live or ___ prerecorded?

What instrumental forces were employed? If live, were where they placed?

_____

_____

Choose a selection from the work (an aria, a song, or an instrumental number), identify it if you can, and describe its musical features below.

Composer: _____

Selection: _____

Melody: _____

_____

Rhythm/
meter: _____

_____

Harmony: _____

_____

Texture: _____

_____

Tempo: _____

_____

Dynamics: _____

_____

Vocal style: _____

_____

Instrumental _____
style:

_____

Mood: _____

Other: _____

What was your overall reaction to the concert?
    ___ enjoyed it a lot   ___ enjoyed it somewhat
    ___ did not enjoy it much   ___ did not enjoy it at all

What did you like about it? _____

_____

What did you not like about it? _____

_____

Other comments: _____

_____

Concert Report 4: Popular Music

Rock group
Solo singer/Instrumentalist
Jazz combo/Ensemble

ATTACH
TICKET
STUB
HERE

CONCERT SETTING

Date of concert: _____

Place of concert: _____

Name of group(s): _____

_____

Did you know about the performer or group prior to this concert?
___ from recordings   ___ from MTV or radio
___ from a friend   ___ did not know

CONCERT MUSIC

What was the makeup (instruments and voices) of the performance?

_____

_____

_____

How would you describe the style or genre of music performed?

_____

_____

Choose a selection from the concert that you can describe below.

Selection: _____

Melody: _____

_____

Rhythm/
meter: _____

_____

Harmony: _____

_____

Texture: _____

Tempo: _____

Dynamics: _____

Vocal style: _____

Instrumental _____
style:

Mood: _____

Other: _____

What was your overall reaction to the concert?
    ___ enjoyed it a lot   ___ enjoyed it somewhat
    ___ did not enjoy it much   ___ did not enjoy it at all

What did you like about it? _____

_____

What did you not like about it? _____

_____

Other comments: _____

_____

_____

Concert Report 5: World Music

Non-Western groups or soloists
World beat

CONCERT SETTING

Date of concert: _____

Place of concert: _____

Name of group(s): _____

_____

Country(ies) or culture(s) represented in concert: _____

_____

Was there a concert program? ___ yes ___ no

Were there any: program notes? ___ yes ___ no

　　　　　　　　spoken remarks? ___ yes ___ no

CONCERT MUSIC

What was the makeup (instruments and voices) of the performance?

_____

_____

_____

_____

What was unfamiliar to you about the music and its performance?

_____

_____

_____

What was familiar to you about it? _____

_____

_____

_____

Choose a selection from the concert that you can describe below.

Selection: _____

Melody: _____

_____

Rhythm/
meter: _____

_____

Harmony: _____

_____

Texture: _____

_____

Tempo: _____

_____

Dynamics: _____

_____

Vocal style: _____

_____

Instrumental _____
style:
_____

Mood: _____

Other: _____

What was your overall reaction to the concert?
___ enjoyed it a lot   ____ enjoyed it somewhat
___ did not enjoy it much   ____ did not enjoy it at all

What did you like about it? _____

_____

What did you not like about it? _____

_____

Other comments: _____

_____

_____

Post-Course Survey

MUSICAL TASTES

Have your musical preferences:

___ changed, ___ expanded, or ___ remained the same?

Which genres did you most enjoy studying?

___ orchestral music   ___ chamber music   ___ opera   ___ musical

___ choral music   ___ ballet   ___ solo vocal music   ___ rock

___ jazz   ___ world music

Rate your general reaction to music of various historical eras:

a. like very much

b. like somewhat

c. do not like very much

d. dislike

___ Middle Ages   ___ Renaissance   ___ Baroque

___ Classical   ___ Romantic   ___ 20th century

List two pieces studied that you enjoyed.

_____

_____

What about them appealed to you? _____

_____

List two pieces studied that you did not enjoy.

_____

_____

What about them did not appeal to you? _____

_____

MUSICAL BACKGROUND

During this course, did you:

___ attend concerts?   ___ If so, how many? _____

___ watch TV broadcasts of concerts?   ___ If so, how many? _____

___ watch videos of concerts?   ___ If so, how many? _____

249

Do you think you will attend more concerts than previously?

___ yes   ___ no   ___ don't know

What type of concerts would you now most enjoy?

_____

_____

Have you purchased any music materials during the course (other than course-required materials)? ___ yes ___ no

If yes, what have you purchased? _____

_____

_____

COURSE ASSESSMENT

What was most valuable about the course content? _____

_____

_____

What was most valuable about the textbook? _____

_____

_____

What disappointments did you have with the course content?

_____

_____

Would you like to take another music course?   ___ yes ___ no

If yes, what focus would you most enjoy?

   ___ music appreciation ___ world music ___ jazz ___ rock

   ___ music theory   other _____

Comments: _____

_____

_____